I'm Living Your Dream Life
The Story of a Northwoods Resort Owner

Michele VanOrt Cozzens

McKenna Publishing Group
Indian Wells, California

I'm Living Your Dream Life
The Story of a Northwoods Resort Owner

ISBN: 0-9713659-0-3
LCCN: 2002105313

First Edition
10 9 8 7 6 5 4 3 2 1

Printed in the United States of America

For Stephanie Rose
You'll live forever in our dreams

Table of Contents

*"If one advances confidently
in the direction of his
dreams, and endeavors
to live the life which he
has imagined, he will meet
with a success unexpected
in common hours."*

Henry David Thoreau

How Did We Do It?

I received a call on the resort line a while back from a fellow who was somewhere in the heart of Wisconsin. Caller ID said the area code was 608, so I picked it up in a hurry and answered in my most professional phone voice. We always take the calls from the 608 area code because that's a place from where people actually book cabins, instead of using our toll free line to treat us like travel agents once they learn the resort is already booked for the date they want next summer.

But as it turned out, this man wasn't the least bit interested in booking a cabin.

"Is this Michele?" he asked.

"It sure is."

"I was just reading about you and your husband in *Midwest Living* magazine," he said. "It was about how you guys quit your jobs and chucked it all for something better."

"The article said that?" I asked in disbelief. My copy of the magazine showed a one-paragraph blurb, a mere listing in an article about vacation resorts in northern Wisconsin.

"Well," the caller continued, "my wife and I are working pretty stressful jobs and we'd like to do what you did. So, I guess I'm just calling to pick your brain because you're living my dream life."

Since we've owned and operated a small Northwoods resort, I've lost count of the number of people who have uttered these words: "You're living my dream life." And at first, this surprised me. Running a family vacation resort had never been on that imaginary list of a hundred things I wanted to accomplish before I died. First of all, it's because I'm not a man. Most of the people who utter the dream life phrase, and then talk about fishing with their dads or following around the resort owner where they vacationed like he was the pied piper, are men. And I don't believe they truly have a dream life planned. I think they're probably unhappy with what they're doing for a living, see what we've done, and want very much to believe that fairy tales do exist. It's the old grass is greener—or in the case of life up North, the snow is whiter—on the other side. These men, like so many I've met over the years, are weekend or evening tinkerers. They officially enter the tinkering phase when they become homeowners. My dad was one. His tinkering site of choice was the garage. Some use basements, other's have special rooms, but all inevitably find a spot to partition off and stash it full of tools and gadgets that get your hands dirty. My husband started in the basement. But in his quest to create a tinkerer's heaven, he branched out by building an 1,800 square-foot, heated garage, which was more than large enough to store all his tools and toys. This, by the way, was in addition to his existing three-car garage with workshop and storage areas.

It's no wonder the occupation of resort owner looks so attractive to tinkering men. To them my husband's work may look more like a large-scale hobby than a real job.

As for the woman's role? In a nationwide epidemic of Martha Stewart envy, some men may believe their wives aspire to be domestic goddesses. I think most women, on the other hand, take one look at me doing my job and run in the other direction. God knows I'm no Martha Stewart. I'm not glamorous, certainly not pampered, and my fingernails are always dirty. I dress up once a week, which is on Saturday afternoon to check-in guests, and the rest of the time I'm dressed like a gardener swearing at the creeping charlie infiltrating my lawns and gardens, or a cleaning lady with the distinct aroma of bleach wafting around me. Sometimes friends drop in while I'm in this mode, hug me and ask "Where's the pool?"

Usually I'm going in five different directions at the same time: chasing

I'm Living Your Dream Life

after my kids, who, once I catch them, cling to me as I run to the phone, or sit at the computer with a tower of paperwork as large as a pile of snow after the plow comes through, or get up to answer the doorbell, or fly up or down the stairs to or from the laundry room while carrying a basket full of bed linens. Of course I also spend a lot of time answering questions posed by people wandering onto the property looking for accommodations or directions, or from guests wanting to know things like whether or not I "work outside the home."

To a lot of people I appear as simply a stay-at-home-mom. What I am instead is a work-at-home mom. Dream life? I don't think so. Truly, it's got to be the worst of both worlds.

The way I see it, working moms get up, get themselves ready, get their kids ready and then take those kids somewhere before going to work. Once they're at work, no one cares whether or not they've got kids. They're dressed, showered and most likely have had time to grab a cup of coffee and a bite to eat before lunch. Then, depending on what their job is, they are paid for doing something useful. The well-paid ones have cleaning ladies and/or nannies to take care of the domestic chores, and the not so well-paid ones spend their off-hours doing all the shopping, cooking, cleaning, bill-paying and kid-rearing. Finding time to relax is always a struggle for this group. There simply isn't time for it.

Stay-at-home-moms—depending on whether or not their kids are stay-at-home-kids—probably have it the best, which is why working moms seem to act a little contemptuous of this set. Telling anyone at a party, for example, that you're a stay-at-home-mom can be a real conversation killer. Some people think stay-at-home-moms are incapable of intelligent, adult talk, because during the day they deal with the loss of adult conversation, the burden of routine, and a genuine lack of appreciation from society. Betty Friedan, who wrote *The Feminine Mystique* when I was a kid, called the home a "comfortable concentration camp" for housewives.

Do you know why that phrase about sitting in front of soaps eating bonbons often comes up during conversations about stay-at-home-moms vs. working moms? It's because, I believe, a woman's dream life involves a certain amount of that bonbon element. What healthy heterosexual woman wouldn't want to fall in love, get married, have a couple healthy children and a successful business or career and then have plenty of time to actually relax? If I had formulated a dream life for myself, I'm pretty sure that would sum it up.

So along comes "superwoman" who tries to have it all. Having a home-based business seems like the perfect solution to the quandary we educated and formerly career oriented moms found ourselves after giving birth. For those of us who couldn't imagine a life as Donna Reed and at the same time couldn't imagine leaving our three-month-old babies in the care of someone else when maternity leave was up and the kid just got to the point of being "fun," it was the only solution.

But it ain't easy.

Working at home, where paperwork mingles with laundry and the telephone doesn't stop ringing in the kitchen full of dirty dishes, makes me wonder daily how I'm ever going to "clear my desk." In spite of two days a week during the summer when my daughters are at a sports program, they're constantly underfoot, needing me or doing whatever they can to get my attention. Usually it's when I'm on the phone answering questions about the resort or standing behind the counter in the shop trying to ring up a sale. It's a good day when I can get out of bed early enough to have a shower and a cup of coffee before the kids get up, and an even better day when I can do these things before the doorbell rings.

When I'm completing paperwork I feel a little like I'm sneaking a cigarette in the girl's bathroom, or trying not to get caught while going out to lunch on a closed campus high school. In other words, I'm constantly looking over my shoulder wondering when I'll be interrupted.

Probably the worst part about not having a "real" job is that people think I don't work. I'd like to believe I make it look so easy that the resort simply runs itself, but I think society still isn't ready to recognize the accomplishments of work-at-home-moms. Recently an old friend introduced me to a woman she had just met, and was very impressed that this woman is a chiropractor. The fact that I am a business owner didn't come up in the introduction.

Prior to becoming resort owners, Mike and I both had "real" jobs. Although we were successful and happy in our careers, neither of us wanted to do what we were doing for the rest of our lives. Simply put, we wanted to do something else. And we wanted to do it together.

We were both twenty-nine years old when we were married in San Francisco. It was the 1980s, and to use the term of the decade, we were a couple of "yuppies." Mike was a stockbroker who spent his days on the trading floor yelling and sweating, and on some days making a lot of money. He wore an ugly purple and orange jacket of his own design and had a business called MikeOptions—pronounced my-cop-shins. Having gone through the stock market channels of working for a few different firms, he went from runner to phone clerk to floor manager to finally, trader. Ultimately he found his niche in trading other people's money, and as an independent floor broker got comfortable—at least for a while.

I was a journalist and just before our wedding quit a busy, high-profile position as managing editor of a meetings and travel publication to take a job with a community newspaper publisher in the East Bay. I didn't know it then, but I was already heading toward a quieter lifestyle. The editor job I quit to plan my wedding had me traveling all over the state of California, spending a lot of solo nights in hotel rooms with nothing but a good book or bad TV. It was fun for the first year or two. I stayed at some of the Golden State's finest resort properties, and always received red carpet treatment by the management. By treating me well they did their part to assure I would write nice things about them. Little did they know I was programmed to write nice things about them so our advertising sales staff would have an easier time selling an ad to accompany the article. Obviously not a pure journalist, discarding the term "objectivity" for whatever term the PR students are taught, I guess I was just a suit-wearing, notebook-toting whore in a hotel room. My unspoken motto was: "I scratch your back, you scratch my publisher's." And about my publisher, she only hired me because she liked my Midwestern accent, and learned to like the fact that I was "the least neurotic person she had ever met." But as she approached menopause, which she did loudly and bitterly, she decided she hated me because I was still in my twenties and the least neurotic person she had ever met. After slapping a dog-eared paperback copy of Barbara Raskin's *Hot Flashes* on my desk one morning with the command to read it so I'd understand what she was going through, she proceeded to make my life miserable with long hours and lots of insults. She suddenly equated me with every twenty-seven year-old girl in Marin County who was responsible for stealing a middle-aged husband from a miserable marriage. Actually, I think she was more concerned that I was trying to steal her company.

One week in the middle of a publication redesign, she decided she had to leave town to visit her daughter. She complemented me, saying I could handle the project without her and that she trusted my decisions, blah-blah-blah. But when she came back (about an hour before deadline), she tried to undo everything I had just done. When I fought her on it, she jutted out her lower lip and said, "Well, you've obviously just taken over!" Then she turned on her patent leather pumps and stormed out of my office. I made the deadline and sent the work to the printer without another word from her. But when I went to say good night she sort of apologized by telling me she was just jealous that I was so young and competent, and that she didn't like the feeling of being dispensable in her own company. I understood and took it in stride. But then she followed by telling me I had the "nicest breasts" she had ever seen. In a matter of minutes she turned me from a successful editor into a pair of tits.

I really hated working for other people.

She certainly wasn't the only lunatic I ever worked for, but with that job

I'm Living Your Dream Life

I got my work published regularly, and I enjoyed researching and writing articles. I like to believe I added a little esoteric flair to the otherwise boring world of meetings and conventions. I also had a lot of input with layout and design, another area in which I had training.

After quitting that job and taking another at the newspaper across the Bay, I started as an independent contractor, doing graphic design and production three days a week. But then my new publisher wanted new computers, and I took the job of bringing the term "state-of-the-art" to the production staff. Then I became friendly with a woman who I fantasized a kindred spirit because she wore the title of managing editor. She worked in the office adjacent to mine. Each morning we shared stories and opinions over cinnamon tea and pumpkin muffins, which I bought from the village bakery just below our offices. Her name was Julie and not only was she in a position of authority, but she was also very smart and nowhere near menopause. While I only got my previous job as managing editor because of a nasal accent, she obviously had a superior education and deserved the title. Every morning when I walked into the office, she hit me with something witty. And even when I didn't get it, I pretended I did and wouldn't rest until I could make sense of her reference—whether it was about Caesar Chavez or Milli Vanilli. Whether or not she saw through me I don't know, but I must have impressed her to some extent because she offered me the chance to write a weekly column for the newspaper's Lifestyle section. And I jumped at the chance.

The only editorial guidelines for the seven-hundred-word column were that what I wrote had to be true and not too political. So, I wrote about my little life in the Oakland Hills and the village known as Montclair. I wrote about my family, my garden, and my friends. I wrote about any idea that came to me in the shower or any suggestion that cropped up in a conversation. And for a while I thought I might become a famous columnist like Anna Quindlen, from the *New York Times*. My mind raced ahead to when I'd move to syndication and later compile a book. Since my picture appeared above the column, a grainy black and white headshot, occasionally I was recognized in Oakland or Berkeley and never hid the fact that I was truly flattered—flattered and surprised. People were not only reading the paper, but also reading me!

I quickly got over believing I had nothing truly interesting to say and I loved that job. I rode high on the horse (checking off this accomplishment on that list of a hundred things) when I received my first piece of hate mail. Unfortunately, Julie had moved on in her career to a daily newspaper across the Bay and I had a new, rather unsympathetic editor. He reveled in the hate mail. He published it in the Letters to the Editor section and told me he agreed with the writer, who among other things criticized my comparing the growing number of HIV diagnoses to the growing number of incidents of broken down cars on the freeway shoulders. I used this analogy because I had taken my first HIV test earlier in the week, and on the same day suffered a tire blowout after dark on Highway 24 near the Caldecott Tunnel.

Even though the letter-writer substantiated my fears and self-doubt, after all who really did care about what I had to say about anything, the wording was vicious and personal. It pretty much said, "in an otherwise useful and informative newspaper, who cares what this woman has to say?" It felt awful having my ill-fitting costume of confidence stripped away and I cried in the bathroom under unflattering fluorescent light. It was a signed letter, but the writer only used initials. So I didn't know whether or not it was a man or a woman. It reeked of man. As for Julie's male replacement, I don't know how he felt about the whole thing after I explained to him that the HIV test I took was part of donating blood for his son, a premature, two-pound baby who happened to need my blood type. I went to another editor at the paper for help, who suggested I explain the real reasons for my analogy—something I failed to do in the first piece—in a follow up column. She was a smart, funny woman named Nancy, and I adored her. She told me Eleanor Roosevelt once said that "no one can make you feel inferior without your consent." So, I wiped my tears, forged ahead and wrote the next column titled "The hand that rocks the writer." I learned that if you put yourself out there you have to be prepared for those who either disagree with you or don't like you. Ultimately, this turned out to be one of my first lessons in the department of "People Can Be Jerks." And again, I didn't know it then, but I soon learned I would have a master's degree in this subject after my first few years of living the dream life as a resort owner.

More on that later.

A nice aspect of the work schedule we had during the California years of our marriage, was that we got to spend the afternoons together. Mike was on New York time for stock market trading and came home each day around 2:00 pm. For the most part I set my own schedule at the paper and did a lot of the work at home. So even though it felt like we didn't get to spend much time together, we did have those glorious afternoons before we went off to softball games or volleyball games, which were a huge part of our social life at the time. And those afternoons were almost always spent on the disc golf course.

Playing disc golf and competing in professional tournaments was our thing. We traveled all over the state of California for weekend tournaments and developed friendships in the disc golf community that felt like family. Mike was one of the early idea men in the sport and dedicated a lot of his time to organizing and running tournaments. He created the Caldecott Open tournament, and came up with the idea for the modern NorCal series, which was partially responsible for an ensuing explosion of tournament play in California.

Disc golf is the game of golf played with a Frisbee. Most disc golf courses consist of eighteen holes, and each hole is usually anywhere from one hundred to six-hundred-feet in length. Players use golf discs to get from the tee pad to the target, which is a steel basket about four-feet high. The player scoring the fewest throws wins. There is a Professional Disc

Golf Association with over 20,000 members around the world, and it's a recreational activity that is growing at a phenomenal rate.

So in spite of our quirky little Frisbee affiliation, we evolved from the yuppie category to the d.i.n.k. category and time flew by. But we hit life in the thirties—or perhaps it was the thirties that hit us—and I realized my athletic years were dwindling. I started getting injuries: a broken thumb from catching a line drive at the pitcher's mound, popped blood vessels in my hands from blocking in coed volleyball leagues, bad knees, bad ankles, broken nails, whatever. I knew in the scheme of things I was still a young woman, but my body insisted I enter a new phase. A new, more grown-up phase. I had gone from the little girl who always had bandages on her knees to the grown woman who came to work each week with a new injury. Not only was it embarrassing, but also it was nearly impossible to use an x-acto knife or type with a cast on my hand. The day one of the sports editors came up to me with a Sharpee marker and wrote the word "ASPERSIONS" across my cast in big, block letters, I realized I had become a bit of an office joke.

I had a revelation on the eve of my thirtieth birthday. While driving home from an evening volleyball game where I had a particularly strong performance, I realized I was about as good as I was ever going to be at that sport. If I had any aspirations to be a volleyball superstar, that boat had long since sailed. Athletically speaking, the drive was all downhill from there. So, I needed a new direction. I don't know if it happens to every woman when she first develops nesting instincts, but things got confusing. While life had been for me always a matter of the here and now, suddenly it became about both the past and the future. Was it the threshold of middle age?

I am a product of the 1970s, which was when ordinary housewives started going to work. At that time, my mother metamorphosed from a stay-at-home-mom to a Kelly Girl, and Gloria Steinem and a female P.E.

teacher at my high school who looked just like her, voiced opinions about equal pay for equal work. As they became my personal heroes, I believed I, too, would go to college, earn a degree and have a career. And of course, some day I would get married, have children and continue that career unscathed. Superwoman was in the womb and I was going to be her. I was going to have it all and all of it was going right on schedule. This wasn't a dream life. This was a normal plan.

"When we have a baby," I said to Mike, "it'll work out great because I can take care of it in the morning while you're at work and then you can take care of it in afternoon when I go to work." And even though I don't remember Mike ever saying he thought that was a good idea, I actually believed this would happen. We didn't give up the birth control right away, however.

Then in the spring of 1992, I received an overseas call from my sister Gayle. She lived in East Africa. Nairobi, to be specific. Shortly after college she relocated to Kenya to join the man who became her husband, who was in the middle of a Peace Corps stint. And while I thought Gayle wouldn't last more than six months without her blow-dryer and her close-knit group of friends, I couldn't have been more wrong. She flourished in Kenya. Soon she was fluent in Swahili, teaching English in a girl's high school, managing a tree farm and a road project, and making friends all across the country.

In 1992, however, when the war in Somalia experienced worldwide attention, Gayle's husband was stationed at a U.N. refugee camp near the Kenya-Somalia border where he managed a population of refugees swelling in size from 1,000 to 50,000 in a matter of weeks. Due to emergency evacuation procedures, spouses were not allowed in the camp. So, Gayle found herself alone in Nairobi with nothing better to do than to call me in California and ask me to come join her.

"Please come," she begged. "We'll have so much fun. I'll show you the whole country." Gayle wanted very much to take her older sister by the hand and show her things she had never seen before—teach her the language, introduce her to new people, new foods, new customs. She wanted to show me the incredible woman she had become. And I was game.

Luckily both my husband and the general manager at the newspaper were very understanding, each saying that if he had the opportunity to go to Kenya for a month he'd take it, too. And I promised to get some interesting material for my column from the experience. Although I don't think my editor cared one way or another, I already knew the title of my first column on the subject: "Out of Oakland."

At first Mike got kind of a long face about the whole thing. But he knew I had my heart set and, well, it was Gayle calling. Gayle and I are about as close as two sisters can be. We're Irish Twins, just over eleven months apart. While we didn't share a womb at the same time, it was close enough to experience the same life—at least for the first seventeen years. To this day we count on each other to fill in the memory gaps of our childhood.

The five-week Kenya experience was the catalyst for me to come back to civilization and find a way to get right back out. I think it started on the trip there. I flew from San Francisco to Vancouver and was supposed to go from Vancouver to Frankfurt. But as it turned out, Germany was in the middle of a four-day-old general strike, and the union had threatened to close one of Europe's busiest airports on the day I was scheduled to arrive. It happened. We got word before the flight that we would land in Luxembourg and then had a choice of what we wanted to do. We could be bused to Frankfurt at no charge, or make other arrangements to get to our final destinations from Luxembourg. There was no indication as to if or when the Frankfurt airport might be back in service.

With a brother-in-law in Paris and a friend in Bern, Switzerland, I toyed with the idea of going to either of those places for a few days to wait out the strike. Instead, however, I opted to take my chances and get on the shuttle bus. I felt the sooner I got to Frankfurt, the sooner I'd be in Nairobi. So, along with the rest of the dazed tourists on a roomy, big-windowed bus, I traveled through the pastoral green hills of Luxembourg, a postage stamp sized country even smaller than Rhode Island. (Prior to that day, I didn't even know that country existed.) And after three hours, we entered the great, gray city of Frankfurt.

These were pre e-mail days, better known as the days of the telex. I found a communications station at the airport and made several attempts to contact my sister in Nairobi to tell her I had run into a slight snag. But I had no luck getting through and grew frustrated. I was tired and hungry, a foreigner in a busy airport with the sound of flight information—cancellations and rescheduling—flipping like a deck of metal cards on huge displays over my head. All the while I carried enough luggage for five weeks in Africa along with an extra suitcase I promised to deliver to the family of a Kenyan man who worked for some friends of mine in San Francisco.

I had entered one of my rooms in hell.

This is when I met a young German man named Wolfgang. He was eager to be of service and struck up a conversation.

"You look like you might need some help?" he asked.

"It's that obvious?" I said.

When Wolfgang led me to a more reliable communications station and got my message through to Nairobi, he became an instant friend. He bought me dinner and helped pass the hours. He, too, was a journalist, but he covered the race car circuit, something I knew nothing about. But like any trained journalist, I listened and learned. He was surprised to learn that I was a writer from San Francisco. "When I saw you from across the room," he said, "I knew you were American. But I thought you were from some place like Montana and that you lived out on a ranch. You've got that outdoorsy look about you, like a lot of American girls."

Even though I was rumpled, smelly and makeup free, I assumed that "outdoorsy look" didn't translate back into German as gamey, and took it as a compliment. I guessed his impression was formed because of what I wore. I had on khaki pants and a red, blanket-print jacket that looked like I had just swiped it off the back of a horse. It was a southwestern look—in style at the time. But I liked the sound of that image: me living out in the country on a ranch. I told him I was on my way to a five-week safari in Kenya and maybe that's what he was sensing.

"Trust me," he said, "they're going to open the airport at midnight. This strike will not go on any longer. There's too much garbage on the streets." Part of the general strike included not only shutting down the airport, but the trash collection as well.

Wolfgang was right. The strike ended and all the long-haul flights were the first to leave. I ended up as one of only six passengers on an airbus, and had three flight attendants all to myself.

When I arrived in Kenya, Gayle had planned quite an adventure. Planning is Gayle's forte. From the time she was old enough to draw, she started designing her future home on napkins or paper towels or any piece of scrap paper she could find. She ran through a thousand pens in bound daily planners compiling lists and outlining more trips and adventures than she could take in one lifetime. For my five-week visit she had almost every minute planned. And it was a safari so spectacular, not even Abercrombie and Kent could match it at five times the cost. Among other places, we stayed at tented camps at Delamere and Mt. Kenya, another on an island of Lake Baringo, and at a posh hotel on the coast at Mombasa. But the place that made the biggest and best impression on me was in Laikipia, at a family-run guest ranch called Lewa Downs.

William Craig and his wife, Emma, ran this 80,000-acre ranch and lived there with their young daughters. William was raised on this property, which his grandfather and step-great-grandfather had acquired in 1922. William joked that after the great-grandfather got the adjoining acreage, he also got the wife. There was once a tented camp there, but the tents had been replaced with charming stone and grass thatch cottages in 1986. They served meals on the bougainvillea-graced terrace of the main house, and had facilities to accommodate a maximum of twelve guests. Everything was done in high style.

In addition to the guest facilities and cattle ranching, the Craigs also had a rug-weaving mill on the property. We toured it one day and found the building filled with happily working Kikuyu women. Some combed and spun the wool, while others washed the freshly spun yarn and hung it to dry. There were two large looms in use; each with four seated women tying knots in what they said was a traditional Ethiopian manner. The rugs, consisting mostly of brown, gray, and tan wools, were absolutely beautiful. Some had landscape scenes of mountains and fever or acacia trees, others had animals or simple geometric designs. Our guest cottage had several covering the slippery cement floors as well as a couple hanging high on the walls. If I had had the money, I would have purchased one.

What impressed me the most about Lewa was the lifestyle it provided for the Craigs. As we sat with them at dinner and shared stories of our travels and our homes, their young daughters listened with fascination. What an incredible education for them, I thought. They asked question upon question about America and our lives there, and were truly interested in our impressions of them and of Africa. They seemed happy and quite at ease.

On our last night there, before the generators were turned off and the lights were out, from my bed I stared at cozy, stone walls and the crackling fire, and quietly thanked the Craigs for creating such a comfortable and welcoming place for my sister and me to stay.

And I thought to myself, this is something I'd like to do.

In my fantasies I wondered if Mike and I could create a little utopia someplace where people came to relax, unwind and enjoy the scenery. Could we give them a taste of something that might improve their lives—if only for a week—and take with them when they left? Could we raise a family and expose our children to a stream of people who would teach them about various places and occupations?

Hey, was I starting to form a dream life?

• • •

The bigger question was: how would Mike feel about changing his lifestyle and operating such a business?

You see, while I aspired to be a country girl who was always fond of the adage, "Live simply so that other's may simply live," my husband was definitely a city boy. Raised in Evanston, Illinois, a city dressed in suburban clothing, Mike loved "the throngs." That's what he called crowds—the throngs. Crowds at concerts, crowds at sporting events, crowds on the trading floor where he worked.

One of those guys who always grabbed the sports section first, he had season tickets for the Golden State Warriors and the San Francisco Giants. When I fell in love with Mike, he was the manager and long-ball-hitter on a men's softball team known as The Dirt Bags. I was a fan in the stands at his games and he helped turn me into a fan in the stands of the Oakland Coliseum and Candlestick Park, as most of our "dates" were centered on these activities. We also attended every Grateful Dead show that came around—and in California at that time, this was a lot of shows. There we moved easily through the colorful crowd, mostly consisting of dancers dressed in rags and bells, with twirling dreadlocks and no regard for personal hygiene. I may have been in a crowd and it may have been loud, but I was barefoot and free and it felt good to be outside and particularly good to be in love with such a beautiful, fun-loving man.

My trip to Kenya was our first separation of any kind. And when I got home I almost didn't recognize him. He had lost fifteen pounds after he started running to pass the time. I think he stopped eating, as well. When I came home bubbling with enthusiasm and talking about a new life, Mike listened. And as it turned out, he had some ideas of his own.

Mike came from a family of sailors. His dad, a former Navy man during World War II, passed down his sailing experience to his sons in the form of star-boat sailing on Lake Michigan. His older brothers took to the activity more than Mike, with one actually winning a gold medal in his class during the 1984 Pan-American games. But Mike had a small boat, a laser, which we often took on camping trips to Lake County in northern California or to mountain lakes in the Sierras. Having spent all my childhood summers on lakes in Michigan and later Missouri, and a true product of YMCA camp, I had some sailing experience as well. The first time Mike handed me the tiller and the line of the mainsail, I took over with confidence and sailed us all around a small reservoir where we spent a lot of time because it was adjacent to a disc golf course.

"Hey," he said, "you're a good little sailor."

"I didn't go to Camp Wakeshma just to meet boys," I said. "Now duck before you get hit with the boom."

One autumn day while sailing on a tarn called Stumpy Meadows in the Sierra foothills, Mike was at the helm while I perched on the faded, lime-green bow. It was technically a one-person boat, so when two sailed creative seating was in order. It was a calm day and the air was warm, but the lake's water was frigid. We sailed slowly back and forth looking for wind and talking about nothing, when without warning a powerful gust hit us. It was so strong that it sent the boom sweeping across the boat with a left hook that punched Mike right into the icy water. At once I flattened to my stomach. With all fours stretched out and clinging like a lizard, I kept the boat from capsizing. The boat sailed about a hundred-feet past Mike before I managed to crawl to the tiller, grab the mainsheet and come-about to rescue him.

It was the first and only time I've ever seen panic in Mike's face. His big blue eyes had full-moon circles of white around them and he splashed around not so much like he was drowning, but more like he was trying to grab onto something that wasn't there. As he breathlessly uttered my name, the second syllable sounded like an exhale, and hearing my name as a synonym for "help me!" was both scary and exhilarating. It took all my strength to haul him and his cold, soaked clothing back into the boat.

We started sailing lessons shortly after that. Each Saturday we traveled from our little house in the hills across the Bay Bridge to the Spinnaker

Sailing School, where our classroom setting was the San Francisco Bay. I loved the feel of my new deck shoes and the briny smell around the docks. Each time I stepped onto the boat, I was ready to use my new vocabulary and take to the sea. But I had a severe case of knot dyslexia. I knew all the names of the knots, but I just couldn't seem to get my rabbit "out of the hole, around the tree, and back into the hole" without the whole thing coming apart. Mike helped me through the sections on bowlines and clove hitches, and we passed the tests. Sailing became as enjoyable an activity for us as disc golf.

Now, this is the part that is sort of unbelievable. I think one of us must have wished on a wishbone or something because almost magically the possibility of operating a boat for charter dropped in front of us. She was called Pocahontas and she was a forty-seven-foot J-boat. The boat belonged to Mike's dad, who had it custom built to use on Lake Michigan between his home near Chicago and his place of business in Milwaukee. He named her Pocahontas because of family ties to the famous Indian maiden. Although I've never met one outside my husband's family, I'm told a lot of Americans claim to be direct descendents of Pocahontas, and the Cozzens' family has a tree and crest drawn up to prove it. It's a pretty standard Celtic crest with the helmet from a suit of armor on top and crowned with a cannon firing a ball. Each side is flanked by a skinny Doberman, and the motto *Bhear na righ gan* waves meaningfully across a red ribbon. Mike always told me it meant "First after me," which I thought was appropriate for his family. But I looked up the real translation, and according to the General Armory of England, Scotland, Ireland and Wales, it really means "May the king live forever."

Meanwhile, Mike's brother Todd, the gold medal holder and employee of Dad's company, had been transferred from an exciting cosmopolitan experience in Paris, France, where he successfully spearheaded the European operation, to the not as exciting city of Milwaukee, Wisconsin. I think the Pocahontas was a lure to get him to stay and take over the reigns at the

26

corporate headquarters. But it didn't quite work. Much the same way Captain John Rolfe took the Indian princess back with him to the Motherland, Todd took Pocahontas back with him to Europe where he started his own company and she stayed in port in the south of France. Except for an occasional race, I think the boat sat unused, soaking up sunrays and mooring fees. So, one day Mike's dad casually mentioned that if we had an interest in the boat and could get it back from Europe, we might want to develop a charter cruising business.

"You'd give us the Pocahontas?" I said to my father-in-law. It was a statement uttered in disbelief more than a question. Where I came from, people didn't just pass around yachts.

"Well I wouldn't just *give* it to you," he bellowed back at me. "We'd have to make a business arrangement."

I was immediately reminded of the year 1980, when I was twenty years old and it was the first time I could vote in a national election. The big race was between Jimmy Carter and Ronald Reagan. But that year I voted for the Citizen's Party candidate, Barry Commoner. At the time I was a junior in college responsible for my own tuition and room and board. I cast my first presidential vote for Mr. Commoner partly because he was associated with the phrase, "there's no such thing as a free lunch." What my father-in-law meant that day was: "there's no such thing as a free Pocahontas." In other words, people *didn't* just pass around yachts.

While my mind raced ahead to a rather Bohemian lifestyle—living aboard the boat in the Florida Keys or some remote island in the Caribbean, I could almost hear the rhythm of the steel drums. I'd be toned and tanned instead of the big red freckle that stared back at me in the mirror, and long blonde streaks—completely natural, of course—would run through the wind-blown tendrils of my hair. That "outdoorsy American girl look" that Wolfgang the race car journalist talked about would really define me. Mike would be the skipper, I'd be his little buddy, and we'd spend our days giving three-hour tours. Yeah mon, it sounded excellent.

But only for a while.

Mike and I contemplated moving up the sailing ladder to the skipper's license program, and even moving to Florida to work on boats to get some experience in the field. But the idea of going into business with the family patriarch seemed less and less attractive. He took the wind right out of my sails by denying me the opportunity to be on the crew if and when the Pocahontas should sail across the Atlantic back to America. "It's no place for a woman," he said. Even though I knew it was more of a protective, fatherly statement than a brutish, chauvinistic statement, I also knew he was right. The idea of living on a boat—not just at sea, but also in port—started to make my legs wobble. It would be just my luck to get seasick and spend the entire trip puking all over the custom teak interior. I also had to admit a fear of storms. After all, we do know what happened to Gilligan on that three-hour tour.

"Do you really think the boat will be a good place to raise a child?" I asked Mike one afternoon at the disc golf course.

No, he didn't. He still hadn't really resigned himself to the child thing yet and that was okay. I wasn't in a hurry. I just wanted to talk about it.

"How about a bed-and-breakfast somewhere," he said while rearranging the discs inside his bag. "We could operate it along with our own disc golf course."

"Wow," I said. "There's an idea that sounds a lot like what I was thinking about in Kenya. It could be a guest ranch."

"A disc golf ranch," said Mike.

"That would be a first," I said. "But I hate to give up on sailing. Can it be on water?"

"It *must* be on water," Mike said. "We can play golf in the morning when it's calm and then sail in the afternoon when the wind comes up."

And there you have it. Considering only the lifestyle and none of the work, we made the decision. Less than six months later we were the new owner/operators of Sandy Point Resort and Disc Golf Ranch.

I'm Living Your Dream Life

So it was a trip to Kenya, a few sailing lessons and a conversation on a disc golf course one afternoon that ultimately led to a new life for my husband and me. And as it turns out, we started a life together that several (many?) consider to be a dream.

Whether or not the following pages propel the fantasy or destroy the myth is a matter of opinion. I don't deny it's been a fun and challenging experience, and I understand why the lifestyle may seem attractive. Some days when the resort is quiet and I'm outside walking on the grounds with the chickadees bouncing from tree branch to tree branch and piercing the clean, cool air with their sharp whistles, I feel so at peace that I believe I'm the luckiest girl alive.

But if you're considering abandoning a busy way of life for a new lifestyle on Golden Pond, please know that owning and operating even a small resort or inn is just plain hard work. It's harder than writing a newspaper column or trading stock options and sometimes, rather than a dream, it can be a nightmare. But, I will say that it's easier than being a parent and more rewarding than working for a demanding and insulting boss. Neither Mike nor I regret the decision.

Oh, and by the way, in case you're a bottom line kind of person, it should be noted that owning a resort like this is not going to make you rich.

The Vision

Here's what we did right: We had a vision. I'm not saying we had a clear-cut vision, but it was a vision and its focus was that we wanted to work together in a mom-and-pop operation. Since we were both already self-employed, we believed we had the motivation to continue on this path. Anyone who has successfully started his own business will cite the shear necessity for self-motivation and the ability to put in countless hours of time. This is one reason why we always chuckle at the dream life statement, because while being your own boss may be attractive and even appear a little bit glamorous, it will always be the hardest job you ever had. Having a business is like having a child. It's always with you.

After giving up on the idea of being charter sailboat operators, our next thought was to buy an inn or a bed-and-breakfast. Mike is a good cook and I like to decorate. So, this made some sense since I could make it look nice and he could make it taste good. Other requirements: it had to be on the water and offer enough land to build a disc golf course, which at a minimum was ten acres. It didn't take us long to realize that because of the high cost of real estate on the left coast these two requirements weren't feasible in the state of California.

So, at the suggestion of Mike's Midwestern brother Jeff, we turned our focus onto the state of Wisconsin. Why Wisconsin? It's a question almost every one of our California friends and associates asked. Not only did many of them not know where Wisconsin was—in fact, one man asked us if it was anywhere near Georgia—but there's some truth to the Eagle's song *Hotel California* where they claim "you can check out anytime you like, but you can never leave." California has something for everyone. There's the ocean, the mountains, the redwoods, the vegetable valley . . . Disneyland. Life there is like one big Grateful Dead Show where the guy on your left is a scientist, the guy on your right is a redneck, and the guy behind you is a freak. And there you are, a face in the crowd who is considered just a "normal person" breathing in lots of fresh air and visual candy, loving the diversity. It seems everyone in the country—and maybe even the world— has an opinion of California, whether or not they've ever lived or even visited there. It isn't for everyone. I spent over a decade living there and had a lot of fun covering the bases of recreational activity and meeting people from all over the world who, like me, migrated there to check out the mystique. But during the time I lived in California, there was no mistaking the crushing feel of an ever-expanding population. If my own personal circle of transplanted friends was any indication of what was happening to the millions of other people in the Bay Area with New York, Baltimore, Atlanta and Chicago accents, I felt that pretty soon the bridges would simply collapse from the weight of the populace. Adding to the mix the earthquake of 1989 and the Berkeley and Oakland Hills fire two years later, a fire that claimed the homes of many of our neighbors, the terra was anything but firma. I shouldn't forget to mention the seven-year drought we lived through where I not only learned to turn off the water while brushing my teeth, but also the catchy little slogan used in the bathroom: "if it's yellow, let it mellow; if it's brown, flush it down." So, after one long party I was ready for some quiet.

I'll never forget the fall of 1992 when we visited Chicago and were at my brother-in-law Jeff's house. One afternoon Mike and I, who were like lost souls, spilled our guts about our ambivalence in getting involved with his dad and the Pocahontas and our desire to get into a different kind of life, which somehow included the game of disc golf. While slumped together on a porch swing, rocking back and forth like a metronome keeping time, Jeff came out with a pair of cold Heinekins. Handing them to us he said, "You know what you guys should do . . . "

I'm Living Your Dream Life

Now, in most cases when someone begins a sentence like that it's time to run. (Many of us are too arrogant to listen to unsolicited advice.) But our posture on that swing certainly begged for advice. And Jeff wasn't just anyone. Standing before us was a caring older brother, a successful neurosurgeon, who I believe is the smartest man I've ever met. (If I'm ever on the Millionaire show he'd be my lifeline.) Further, he had nothing to gain or lose by telling us what he thought we should do with our lives.

He continued, "You two should go look at land in northern Wisconsin."

"I've never been up there," I said. "Is it like Michigan?"

"Even better. It's just beautiful," Jeff said wistfully. A serene look covered his usually serious face and as his eyes looked beyond us toward the sky, memories of past and even recent vacations in the Northwoods played like videotapes in front of us.

"When we were kids, we drove up to Manitowish Waters from Chicago every summer and stayed in a small cabin right next to the lake," he said. "Those were some of the best times about growing up because we felt so, I don't know, so free. We fished. A lot. And we learned how to water ski, too. You remember Rest Lake, don't you Mike?"

Mike, who is seven years younger than Jeff, didn't have as vivid memories of Rest Lake as his brother since he was still pretty young when their family ultimately lost the lease to the land where the cabin sat. The property was owned by the Wisconsin Department of Natural Resources, and the Cozzens family simply paid the property taxes in order to use the cabin. After a ninety-nine year lease, the DNR reclaimed the land. Sparking my husband's memories are black and white photos of himself with white blond hair and striped swim trunks sitting inside a wooden canoe, or holding up a string of walleyes like a giant smile in front of his skinny body.

"I remember the cabin," he said. "It was a log cabin but the logs were vertical instead of horizontal and it was really dark inside because of all the pine trees surrounding it. It had a small kitchen and a screen porch facing

33

the lake with two doors that banged shut. I remember my mom there and I remember that my brother Todd cut his foot while trying to catch crayfish."

The town of Manitowish Waters, which is a forty-minute drive from our resort, remains on the map as a small tourist town just off the main highway with some of the same businesses still in operation since the 1950s and early 1960s when Mike's family vacationed there like the hardware store and the Pea Patch saloon. Unfortunately, the Cozzens' cabin didn't have the same longetivity and now exists only in memories, photos and a few red bricks from the outdoor fireplace that are hidden in the brush where the cabin once stood. The same site is now home to a boat launch and public park.

"I still take my family up North every summer for a vacation," said Jeff. "We stay at a lodge and my kids do all the same things we did."

"We spent our summer vacations on a lake in Michigan," I said. "And you're right, those memories are pretty magical."

"Right!" Jeff almost yelled. "So why don't you sell your house in California and buy a small resort," he said. "There's a ton of them up there and you could build your disc golf course or have sailboats or do whatever you want."

"Okay," we answered in unison. We were easy. The truth is, Jeff spoke with such passion that the joyful memories he and Mike shared took me back to the summers of my own youth, which were spent on Cory Lake in Three Rivers, Michigan. These special weeks at the lake helped shape my childhood: Hours upon hours spent swimming; learning to water-ski behind our dad's wooden Milocraft boat with the maroon forty-horse Johnson motor; catching lightening bugs; using inner-tubes to slide down the hill in front of the cottage we rented; collecting wildflowers and silver dollar bouquets; putting on skits for the grown-ups by the campfire; playing the card game "spoons" and swinging from the vines on the trees in the forest. Whenever I returned to our suburban neighborhood after time spent at the lake, I dreamily looked out my bedroom window toward the grayness of Bartlett Avenue, squinted my eyes and imagined it to be water.

There was no doubt that I loved the lake. But did that make me a qualified candidate for being a resort owner?

Mike and I considered what it might take to be resort operators. First, we liked to be on vacation. Who didn't? But would we like to be in the position of providing a facility for others to enjoy their vacations? Without question, our answer was, "yes." And at the time, according to the national directory of disc golf courses, Wisconsin only had four or five courses in the entire state and none of them were north of Appleton. We felt it might be a good time to introduce the sport to a new territory.

So, we finished our beers and made plans to rent a car the next day. From Chicago we drove north.

Here are some questions we asked ourselves while we drove:

Were we ready to commit to a whole new lifestyle?

Were we ready to give up the throngs of city life, restaurants, concerts, sporting events and cultural diversity in general?

Could we work together as business partners in an isolated environment?

How did we feel about working with the public?

Did we have the energy to do this?

Could we make this work?

Was the Northwoods ready for the game of disc golf?

Was the Northwoods ready for us?

Again, the answer to all of our questions was "Absolutely!"

Though it wasn't the part of Wisconsin Mike's brother suggested, the first place we looked was Door County, the area known as the "thumb" in Wisconsin. Michigan may have dibs on the mitten analogy since the lower part of that state truly is shaped like a mitten, but looking at Wisconsin is a little like looking at the palm of your right hand. The thumb, bordered by Green Bay to the west and Lake Michigan to the east, is a skinny strip of land and a popular tourist destination. The key word here is "skinny." The base of the thumb is about thirty miles across at its widest point, and the land narrows down to a well-filed nail at the tip. Not only was there not enough land to be had to construct a disc golf course, the land that was available was too expensive. It was like California all over again.

We, by the way, had a budget and promised to stick to it. We didn't want to spend more than what we could sell our house for in the Oakland hills; however, that still put us in a good financial position. Our little, two-bedroom, one-bathroom California cottage built on a piece of land measured in inches instead of acres had all the benefits of a California zip code. Real estate prices in California were a lot higher than in the Northwoods, and we could probably afford to buy some land and a business and have change left over to support us while still in the start-up mode. So, after only one night at a cozy little resort on Green Bay, we continued further north.

I had never seen northern Wisconsin prior to this trip. Even though I, too, spent the first seventeen years of my life in the Chicago area, after our family gave up the vacations in Michigan we went south to Missouri. We called it "Misery," because the summers were sweltering. My dad called it God's Country and the land of no mosquitoes. It was where my parents eventually retired. I had spent some time at a friend's cottage in southern Wisconsin near Lake Geneva during high school, but Lake Delevan was as green as pea soup that summer. So, it wasn't as nice as Michigan. At the time, however, the drinking age in Wisconsin was eighteen and that was more attractive than anything. When I was still sixteen and seventeen my friends helped me paint brown eye shadow above my very blue eyes and I tried to pass off the no-photo fake I.D. of our high school's former homecoming queen, saying I was nineteen with brown hair and brown eyes. Sometimes it worked, and I thought going to bars and looking for cute guys was a sophisticated form of entertainment. That made Wisconsin a pretty cool place to hang out. But that was Southern Wisconsin—the Chicago suburbs on vacation. Northern Wisconsin was all new territory for me. And as

I'm Living Your Dream Life

it turned out, timing was everything.

It was October.

October is the time of year when Wisconsin really shows off. The locals in the Northwoods call it "Colorama," and once you've experienced it you wouldn't be tempted to name it anything else. The colors were so vivid; they literally took away my breath. The predominant color was yellow due to the birch and poplar trees whose leaves turn blindingly yellow in the fall. But I gasped each time we passed a red maple tree, with leaves so red only more colorful words like cerise or crimson, maybe vermilion, can describe them. Some maples were also yellow, but still others were as orange as the setting sun. And as we drove through the narrow winding roads passing lake after lake, it was as if the sixty-four-count box of Crayola crayons had just spilled before me. Punctuating all this vivid color was a variety of evergreens, mainly balsam, red and white pine, and cedar. But what made the pallet unique was the tissue-paper, white bark of the birch trees. The birch trees are northern Wisconsin's exclamation point.

With one stroke of its artistic brush, the Northwoods had painted me hooked.

We stopped in the town of Rhinelander, which is the biggest city around and the county seat of Oneida County. It was close to 5:00 pm, so we needed to get to a real estate office in time to find listings of properties for sale. And as luck would have it we spotted a big, plain sign reading "Rhinelander Realty" right on the main drag. We pulled up and waltzed inside.

"We'd like to buy a resort," I announced to the receptionist.

Without a word but with a friendly smile, she got up and disappeared into the offices and cubicles behind her. And within a minute a young woman came out, introduced herself and took us back to her office.

"So, you'd like to buy a resort," she said.

She was new. Her name was Barb and she had only been a real estate agent for about an hour. We couldn't help but think that the receptionist was feeding her what she thought might be a learning experience. We definitely looked like a pair of kids, wearing blue jeans and innocent yet earnest expressions. Both Mike and I look a lot younger than we are. I think it's due to my long wavy hair and freckles and Mike's baby face and baseball cap. But we were serious about our plan, and Barb took us seriously right from the start.

It took her about half an hour to print out a long list of available properties in the area, with a minimum of six acres and a maximum of forty acres. The price range went from $150,000 to $450,000. We thanked her and took her recommendation to stay at a nearby Best Western Hotel.

That night featured one of the presidential candidate debates on television between Bill Clinton and the first George Bush. I remember spreading out the MLS listings in front of the TV, along with a giant map of the area covering several towns including Rhinelander, Three Lakes, Minocqua, Arbor Vitae, Woodruff, Manitowish, Lac du Flambeau—about a fifty-mile radius. Then I went to work.

I narrowed down the listings to ten properties and marked a veritable treasure map for us to follow so we could visit each property the next day.

Most of the first eight properties were dumps. Buildings were rotting or falling down and garbage was strewn about. We didn't even want to get out of the car. Two or three were okay, but there wasn't enough space for the disc golf course. It seemed there was something wrong enough with each one to cross it off the list. So we kept driving, with Mike at the wheel and me beside him with my face buried in the map. Every place we stopped we were treated well and found the people to be quite friendly. I was convinced that everyone in Wisconsin was a nice person—a nice person with a funny accent.

"Want a baaaag, do ya?" asked the clerk at a mini-mart in Three Lakes where I picked up some orange juice.

As we headed west into the afternoon, we drove past Minocqua and into Lac du Flambeau. This is where we saw the first property with real potential. It was a resort located on a big lake and sat on twenty acres. The owner's house was certainly a place where we could live and the cabins, while not in the best shape, had potential to be nice with a little TLC. So we stored that resort in our possibilities file and moved on to the tenth and final property.

"One more," I said to Mike. "The last one is pretty close and it has the most land. Forty acres and five cabins, plus a year round house for the owners. And guess what? The asking price is in range: $240,000."

And that's when we saw Sandy Point for the first time.

Turning south off of Hwy. 70, we came across the sign for the resort and then turned onto Sandy Point Lane. It was a narrow dirt road about a quarter mile long, with trees reaching across to form a covered bridge of colorful leaves. And at the end of the road we parked in front of a large, chalet-style home and got out slowly. As smoke smoldered through the chimney and circulated like a cloud in the front yard, we figured someone was inside enjoying a fire on such a beautiful autumn day. But when we rang the doorbell, which buzzed as loud as a time-out horn at an NBA basketball game, no one answered. We rang again. No answer. Obviously no one was home.

Aside from saying it was strange that someone left a fire burning, Mike and I didn't speak. He looked toward the lake. I looked toward the lake. Then we looked at each other and nodded, and headed in that direction like we were off to see the wizard. A wide path of railroad-tie steps led us to the waters of Squaw Lake, while charming little brown cabins poked out from behind the trees. A soft breeze from the south blew my hair behind me as we walked to the end of an eighty-foot, redwood stained dock, where we stood and stared at the rippling water. The lake was about a mile wide from our vantage point and looked long and narrow like a river. The shore-line was thick with trees and very few homes or cottages were visible. There were no boats and no activity other than the sound of lapping waves softly hitting the dock and the shore behind us. We turned to each other, smiled, and like Brigham Young to his group of Mormon followers when he first saw Salt Lake said, "This is the place!"

Most of the cabins were unlocked, and like guilty trespassers we quickly and cautiously looked inside as the shadows grew long. We still had a six-hour drive back to Chicago, with a flight back to California in the morning. "Cute, cute, cute," is what I said upon entering each cabin. There was lots of knotty-pine paneling and mismatched furniture. And they were very clean. Mike didn't say much, but his expression—raised eyebrows and closed lips stretched tight across his face—suggested he was impressed.

"You're kidding," said Barb when we called her from a pay phone on the side of the road to tell her we found the place we wanted to buy.

In the next two months Barb made arrangements for us to tour and inspect each cabin, as well as the owner's house. She enabled us to meet with the owners, who provided a wealth of information about not only the property, but also about the business. Through our negotiations we requested that part of the deal be a series of "teaching sessions" where the owners basically showed us how to be resort operators. This was another thing we did right.

The soon-to-be former pop of their mom-and-pop operation showed Mike where the septic systems were located and explained his annual process of winterizing each cabin by draining the water heaters and underground pipes. He pointed out all the changes and additions he had made during his eight-year tenure as owner, showed us several unfinished projects, and had all kinds of suggestions for how we might tackle repairs and future projects.

"You know what I would do," he started everything he said by saying that opening remark. "You gotta make these cabins year-round units. There's a lot of winter business to be had with all the snowmobilers. But be sure to charge them a damage deposit. They'll take apart their sleds and clean the greasy parts right on your carpets."

Asked why he was getting out of the resort business he said, "I'm sick of people wrecking my stuff."

Meanwhile, the mom told me about her Saturday cleaning routine and showed me where she stored the bed linens and curtains.

"My daughter said I shouldn't label the boxes of curtains just to make you guess where they belonged," she confessed. "But I figured you have enough to deal with, so I labeled them for you. There's so much junk up there for you to go through. All of the previous owners left their linens."

She also kept track of all the bookkeeping and reservations, and shared her systems with me. This woman, while very nice to me and with my best interests at heart, approached her lessons with how everything had gone or could go wrong.

"Be sure to make a deadline for reservation deposits," she suggested. "And stick to it. I don't want to mention any names, but you'll always have guests who tell you they're sending it in and then never do. Meanwhile you're turning away a bunch of people."

I wanted her to mention names. Truly, I wanted the dirt. But she, in a very tactful manner, didn't want to taint my opinion of any of the guests before I had the opportunity to like or detest them on my own.

Over the next few years, whenever I ran into her in town and she asked about the business, we found we shared the same opinion of the guests we had in common. We liked and appreciated the same people and disliked the same ones as well. "I had been trying to find a way to get rid of them for years!" she said about one rowdy and destructive group who found another place to stay the following summer after a week with us as intolerant hosts. And what's even funnier about that is I know the owner of the resort where they took up residence, and she can't stand them either. Resort owners do have ways of sharing guest stories and getting each other through the rough spots. It's like an informal Resort Owners Support Group.

When the previous mom-owner of Sandy Point was asked why she was getting out of the resort business she said, "I never really wanted to do this in the first place. We were living in another state when my husband came back from a trip up here one day and he told me he bought a resort." After talking with her some more, I gathered it was tough on her, too, having people abuse the surroundings. Her cabins were spotless and her home immaculate. She made us take off our shoes—snow boots actually—when we entered the cabins to officially view them for the first time, and I sensed her eyes darting to the rafters as she instinctively looked for cobwebs or other signs of imperfection. She also admitted that she didn't care to socialize with the guests.

I wondered how *we* would feel about this part of the job.

One thing I knew for sure was that Mike and I are indeed social people—an absolute requirement for the resort business. Mike spent his days on the trading floor surrounded by over five-hundred other people, all of whom yelled back and forth to each other for seven hours a day. He knew almost everyone on a first name basis. And Mike was popular. People just like Mike. When my mom used to refer to Mike's popularity, she'd say that people tend to know a "good time when they see one." And Mike is nothing if not a good time.

I, too, was accustomed to working in people-oriented environments. As an editor in the meetings and conventions industry, I attended several functions each week and unabashedly approached interesting looking people to sniff out a story for our publication. I learned how to get people to talk to me and found I was usually interested in what they had to say. As for people liking me, I can only say it's a mixed bag. Generally, older people and those more intelligent than I either like or are amused by me. Younger people, like my nieces and nephews or the kids I coach on the soccer field, often look at me like I'm goofy. Others either treat me like I'm a lot smarter than I am or tend to make no secret of hating me. Ultimately, I've found a pretty large circle of friends who, age aside, seem to be just like me—neither smart nor stupid—but just going through the motions and learning along the way. By the way, my very smart sister Debra taught me to believe that your opinion of me is none of my business.

I'm Living Your Dream Life

The previous owners of Sandy Point informed us that the following summer season was about sixty-five percent booked with reservations they had with former customers. They assured us that the summer would fill up, as they typically turned away requests for bookings each year. This made it rather simple to develop a business plan by predicting income and basing our expenses on the past tax returns they provided.

We studied the statistics on resort expenses such as propane and electricity, telephone, postage, cleaning supplies and trash disposal. Office expenses and advertising were minimal during their tenure, but the costs of insurance and maintenance and repair were higher than we expected. Their children were their only employees and they paid very little for other outside services. Still childless, it was about that time when I first wished I could give birth to a sixteen-year-old boy to help with the chores around the resort.

Because they operated Sandy Point as a tax write-off, in other words at a loss, made us accept that we had our work cut out for us. Like some resort owners in the Northwoods who only concentrate on the summer tourist season, they had other jobs with the local school systems, which freed up their summers to work the resort. We had no intention of obtaining other jobs and hoped to operate the resort as a profitable and sustaining operation.

Another thing we did right: We had enough money to support us for about five years while we turned Sandy Point into a profitable business.

Buying an established resort had several advantages, but it also presented several challenges. Sandy Point had existed as a family vacation facility since the mid-1930s. The original owners, The Andersons, built each of the five cabins on the property from cedar trees harvested from the surrounding acreage. This meant that they had a lot of classic charm, but it also meant that they were quite old.

The cabins were small, about five-hundred square-feet each. And while a typical log cabin like the logo pictured on bottles of Log Cabin syrup might come to mind, these traditional Northwoods cabins were vertical instead of horizontal. Like Mike's childhood cabin on Rest Lake, they consisted of narrow cedar logs about six to eight inches in diameter, which were split in half and vertically placed side by side. The rounded portions made up the outside walls of the cabin, and the flat, rough-sawn interior of the log made up the inside paneling. The tall, cathedral ceilings were paneled with beautiful cedar planks coated in heavy varnish, and the exposed beams were full, cedar logs. Really, the ceilings were the prettiest parts of these cabins.

The original cabins were only equipped with bedrooms. Each had its own outhouse and guests bathed at a centrally located shower facility and took their meals at the main house where the Anderson's lived. The cabins had folksy names like, "Uneeda Rest," and "Seldom Inn." The smallest was named "Honeymoon," while the largest was "The Big House." And the fifth was named for its location, which was "Hilltop." By the time we inherited the cabins they were simply named numbers one through five, and we didn't learn the original names until about a year after we bought the resort. A series of former owners have stopped in over the years to see the place, introduce themselves and share stories and photos of their lives at Sandy Point.

Giving the cabins new names was one of the first things we did after redecorating. As the new owners, it was our turn to make a mark.

Cabin One, or Uneeda Rest, the closest to the lake and the one with the most charm, was named "Karibu," pronounced ka-reé-boo. Karibu means "welcome" in Swahili. I wanted to bring the African inspiration into play and with my sister's help, decorated it with tribal artifacts and put mosquito nets over the beds. In my experience there were far more mosquitoes in northern Wisconsin than in the deepest bush or even rain forests of Kenya. But at least Wisconsin mosquitoes didn't pose the threat of malaria. So, the nets, while functional, simply added an aesthetic touch. "Stay in Karibu for your Northwoods safari."

I'm Living Your Dream Life

We named Cabin Two or Hilltop, "Zeke's Lair." We learned from the children of the previous owners that a little bear lived near the resort and each spring when he arose from a long winter's hibernation, found his way to the porch of this cabin. We never saw the bear but named him Zeke anyway. Old Zeke to be more precise. Having just spent so many years in and around Berkeley, California and on the University of California campus where there's a student gathering place called the "Bear's Lair," I stole the name.

Cabin Three, Seldom Inn, was easily named. We called it "Wolf Den," and this was because of Luna and Dakotah. Luna and Dakotah were our wolf pups, who we adopted only three weeks after moving to Wisconsin. The black labs we had when we first married had both passed away a year or so before we moved, and we were ready to find some new canine companionship. These hybrids, a cross between arctic and timber wolf, German shepherd and husky, were adorable and yet very challenging. Wanting to always run free and avoid captivity, they found comfort on the steps of Cabin Three as well as in the holes they dug underneath it. It was their cabin. Luna, who was always more wolf than dog in personality, actually ran off after a series of summer thunderstorms in 1998, and we never heard from her again. Since she was an exquisite, pure white beauty reminiscent of the lead sled dog in the movie *Iron Will*, we like to believe someone found her as lovable as we did and adopted her. Either that or she's running wild with a pack somewhere in the great Northwoods. As for Dakotah, because we now live in the desert during the winter (which is no climate for this breed) these days she lives with our best friend in the Sierra foothills outside of Nevada City, California. We, of course, have visiting privileges and she's always happy to see us.

Cabin Four, formerly known as "Honeymoon," was renamed "Ivan's Lure." And this happened because of an old friend of Mike's named Jay, who was also from Evanston. Jay was looking for work just when we needed a hand—literally. Right after moving to the resort Mike developed carpal

45

tunnel syndrome and required surgery. When one suddenly takes a man off the trading floor and puts a hammer in his hand, it's bound to happen. This put him out of commission for several weeks when the resort was in need of all the regular spring maintenance and the touches we wanted to give it as new owners. Jay was a colorful character, who looked a lot like the actor Judge Reinhold, the goony detective in the movie *Beverly Hills Cop*. He worked hard and kept us entertained. Mike called him "Jay-Bo." Later his nickname evolved to "Jay-Boeski." Then Ivan Boeski after the high-profile Wall Street financier. And finally it was just Ivan. While fishing one day Ivan lost his favorite muskie lure and we never heard the end of it. Ivan's lure became the topic in almost every conversation we had with him.

"I'm looking for a piece of fruit. And man, I can't believe I lost that lure."

On the day he painted cabin number four, moaning about his lure with each stroke of the brush, we decided to call the newly updated cabin "Ivan's Lure."

As for Cabin Five, formerly known as the "Big House," we named it after the Northwoods mascot, the loon. Commonly known as the common loon, we called the cabin the "Uncommon Loon" just to be different. But it was certainly an uncommon dwelling.

Previous owners throughout the decades had updated the cabins to include bathrooms and full kitchens and there were patchwork signs of each generation of owners. Each cabin had a crazy quilt-like quality. Crazy quilts are a sort of quilt genre, which grew in popularity during the early 1900s. Now collector's items, they were put together with scraps of mismatched fabrics and had no real pattern. Cabin Five had five different kinds of paneling. In the kitchen a layer of paneling from the 1980s covered some blue Formica-type material from the 1970s, which covered contact paper that looked like a pattern from Goldie Hawn's bikini while she danced on the Laugh-In television show in the 1960s. We stripped away layer upon layer to get back World War II and the Depression—in other words, back to the cedar.

In all the cabins the water heaters were rusty and had temperamental pilot lights. The bed mattresses were shaped like lazy smiles. The curtains were faded and the bed linens pilly. And whoever brought electricity to the units was lucky he didn't have a fire on his hands. There were exposed and fraying wires without junction boxes or grounded receptacles, and everything in each cabin was plugged into one or two outlets. It was no wonder why these cabins didn't have coffee pots and microwaves.

Our original business plan allotted for some updating, but not as much capital as we ultimately put into each unit. Buying a bunch of cabins built in the 1930s was like "This Old House" on steroids. It took a lot longer than a half-hour inspection segment to determine all the needs, and until we bought the place and could really get inside we truly had no idea of the hornet's nest of repairs and updates in store. So, we approached the cabin redecorating and updating process with an open-ended budget. We admit when we first saw the resort we were sucked in by its charm, and didn't fully examine all the details that would end up costing us a great deal of money.

So, brushing naiveté aside, our vision simply became more grand. We planned for each cabin to become a place where *we* would spend a week. At the time each rented for and was worth $400 per week, which is the rate the former owners set for the summer of 1993. The cabins we wanted to own, however, would be worth much more. Considering we had to make enough money to operate the business and support us, we had no choice.

We started by adding two additional units that were year-round, log-sided homes. Now, neither Mike nor I had ever built a house before, but we were willing to give it a try. The only previous construction experience we had was with remodeling—or tinkering—projects in our home in California. This included installing hardwood floors and some bathroom and kitchen tile work. Not exactly the qualifications for building a nine-hundred square-foot cabin from scratch, but what did we really know about anything? So, like true beginner tinkerers we bought a kit and followed the directions. It's a miracle that the first cabin we built—the one where we made all our rookie mistakes—is still standing. But it is, and unless we point out the errors most people never notice them.

Building was fun. I liked wearing a tool belt. And even though I couldn't seem to find a way to keep the hammer from beating me in the legs when I walked, with practice I managed to at some point stop imitating a carpenter and start hammering like one.

Completed in May of 1994, the new cabins were a huge hit with the guests. The first to stay in them were long-time guests of the resort, a family who had been vacationing at Sandy Point since the 1930s. And while I worried that they might miss the old cabins, units they knew more about than we did when we first became owners, they were delighted with the upgrade. "This is as nice as our home," said one of the men.

We found a big demand for "nice cabins." Of course people want clean facilities, but baby-boomers want and are willing to pay for amenities. Old Northwoods cabins may be as interesting to look at as collectible muskie lures, but when it comes to really catching that fish or housing your family for a week, customers—especially women—want something modern.

A lot like the notion that we're living the dream life of more men than women, I discovered as well that a vacation cabin in the Northwoods was more often than not a "daddy idea." While daddy had the vision of reliving his youth with his own kids at the lake, and believe me we've heard this story a hundred times, mommy's idea of a vacation doesn't include bugs, cooking, cleaning or chasing after the kids. The fact that Sandy Point offers "housekeeping units," which means they're clean when guests arrive but staff doesn't go in on a daily basis to wash dishes and make beds, requires compromise from the mommies. So when they call to make the reservations (because planning is almost always the mommy's job), they make it clear that they want the closest thing to the Ritz they can afford.

With the mommies in mind I paid special attention to the bed linens, and invested in quilts for all the beds. The previous decor, which included things like dogs playing poker; chicks, ducks, geese, and Jesus Christ on black velvet, was removed and replaced with items pertaining to a theme around the cabin name. I attended auctions and haunted local antique stores, looking for old fishing poles, lures and creels—anything with some vintage Northwoods flavor. It was helpful that sources like Spiegel catalog were currently featuring a lodge-look style of decor.

The other enormous task awaiting us after we redecorated the cabins was construction of the disc golf course. Realistically we knew it would be a few years before we had anything close to a world-class course. This was because of the trees. The forest on our property was so thick with poplar saplings and underbrush you practically needed a machete to walk through it. Every hike was an effort in trail-blazing.

Before our first season began we attended a Chamber of Commerce sponsored workshop for resort owners, where a small group sat around and shared ideas in a round table discussion. Introduced as the new kids on the block, they welcomed us to the fold.

"You can tell they're new," someone said. "They're still smiling."

"We hear you're going to build some kind of golf course."

"Yes, that's right," said Mike. "It's a *disc* golf course."

"Disc golf? What on earth is that?"

"Golf played with a Frisbee," I said.

"And you're going to build it, uh, where exactly?"

"On the property."

"*That* property?" they laughed. "Impossible!"

We knew they had never heard of disc golf and could only imagine the wide green fairways of a typical ball golf course. While many disc golf courses offer the opportunity for long, open shots, many are forested with trees as key obstacles. You know how miniature golf courses have statues and windmills to negotiate and ball golf courses have lakes and sand traps? Well, disc golf courses have trees. And our course was going to have lots of trees. Ironically, neither Mike nor I were particularly fond of accuracy courses, but figured with the course we were about to create we'd have plenty of opportunity to work on that aspect of our game.

Without an aerial view of the property, we had to study and survey the land on foot and try to visualize stringing together the fairways. We planned to design a classic course with nine holes out and nine back in. I had no idea where to start, but Mike sure did. An avid disc golfer who had played hundreds of courses for over twenty years, he had a vision of what he wanted from the very beginning. I thought he was like the Robert Trent Jones of the disc golf world.

He started with what he called the natural fairways, which were the power-line right-of-ways. There are two distinct overhead power line clearings running through the property. Each is a twenty-five foot grass path lined with walls of trees. One of them, now hole eight, has become our signature hole. It's the longest one, measuring three-hundred fifty-four feet, and the tee pad is elevated. The ground immediately drops off to a little valley, and then rises again toward a basket that's at about the same elevation as the tee pad. And while I've seen some of the top pros who have played our course put the disc right under the basket on their drive, this is a pretty tough hole because of the narrow fairway. If you release the disc too early, or over-crank and let go too late, you'll end up in the trees. That's a guaranteed hunt. During our tournaments we always hire a spotter to sit in the valley to help play move along more smoothly.

When it came time to create the front nine—or the eight other holes to connect to hole eight—the course evolved one hole at a time. We let the big trees be our guides. We didn't want to sacrifice any big trees and worked the fairways around them whenever we could. We welcomed input. Several friends, who happened to be golfers, showed up during our first months' of operation to see what we were up to and offer support.

"Where are you going to put the course?" they asked with a mixture of excitement and skepticism when seeing all the trees.

I'm Living Your Dream Life

"I've got a general idea," said Mike, "but you're welcome to design a hole if you like."

Most golfers jump at the chance to have input on course design. And our course was no exception. For example, the world distance record holder at the time, Scott Stokely, designed our original hole number one. And the funny thing is it was the shortest hole on the course. It was a nice way to start the game for both beginners and pros because it was short and definitely aceable. There's nothing like starting out your round with an ace.

Little by little as the word got out around the state that a new course was going in, golfers dropped by to check out the site. We offered golfers the chance to act as work crews in exchange for free cabins. Several different groups over the years have come to the resort to get away, play a little golf, swim or fish and put in time trimming brush and clearing fairways. It was a great deal for us.

As for the equipment, we started economically by purchasing a new basket design called the "pole-hole light." The Disc Golf Association and Ed Headrick who "invented" the sport of disc golf, based the design on his classic pole-hole design. But the poles running up the middle were half the thickness, and therefore about half the price. We're talking two hundred dollars each for eighteen holes as opposed to four-hundred. It was a start, but it didn't make us a world-class course. Eventually we sold the baskets to a man who managed a camp in Vermont and purchased another new design called the Mach Fore. But this new design still didn't do the trick for us, especially when the course evolved to twenty-two holes (and twenty-four for tournaments), and hosted two well-attended events each year. We sold the second set of baskets to the same man in Vermont and finally purchased the industry favorite, the DGA Mach Three, which remain in the ground today. Ultimately, the new equipment cost us in excess of $10,000.

As the course caught on in popularity, we started charging a green fee to the public. First it was two dollars for all-day play, including the use of golf discs, but escalated to four-dollars with no charge for kids under twelve. (Still a darn good deal for some good, clean family fun.) The year we constructed our pro shop, which saw its first full season of operation in 2000, golfers came in off the street nearly every day from May until September. We never dreamed the green fees we collected would some day pay for the equipment, but that day will come in just a few more years.

And our fellow Chamber members laughed and told us it couldn't be done.

On that note, joining the Minocqua-Arbor-Vitae-Woodruff Chamber of Commerce was another thing we did right. It's an extremely well-run organization with a popular website and a slick visitor's guide that goes out to around 100,000 people per year. Tapping into their huge advertising budget for the price of membership is a really good deal. Plus, the staff is a particularly nice group of people. They visit the resort from time to time just to check out the property and see the changes first hand, so that they can recommend our facility with confidence to some of the 200,000 callers who ring their phones looking for accommodations each year. We credit the Chamber for helping to make our business a success.

While the vision of operating a family resort remains in tact, it took us eight full seasons before we saw our first minuscule profit. And instead of surging forward and watching the bucks roll in, it's been hard to stop improving. Take the day Mike ran into the local paving company in the process of resurfacing the road leading to our lane. He wanted to have our quarter-mile lane paved from the beginning and couldn't resist taking advantage of the opportunity.

"Hey, since you guys are already out here with your equipment, how about a discount on my road?" he asked. We received the discount, but it was still another sixteen grand spent on asphalt that I hoped would be a different form of black gold—or profit. Ultimately, it was a good move. Each previous season we had the chore of finding someone to grade the dirt road and add the gravel which ended up clinging to the undersides of cars with Illinois license plates heading south on departure day. It's also kept down the dust levels and makes the place look cleaner. At first we were nervous about changing the natural, rustic appeal of the entrance, and thought we might have to rename Sandy Point Resort to "Asphalt Point Resort." But that wasn't the case. As each improvement makes the unimproved areas look worse, we may need to pave the remaining roads as well.

Improvements are addictive, and the cabins are another example. After building the new ones, the older ones seemed, well, smaller, older, dirtier, smellier, and less attractive to the customers. As a result, upon entering our ninth summer season we had only one of the original five cabins remaining. Karibu. It stands in its original position (the closest cabin to the lake) like a museum piece.

The first of the original cabins to go were the Wolf Den and Ivan's Lure. We knew Ivan's Lure was at the end of its life. It was so small that the bathroom was the size of an airplane lavatory, and the living room the size of a loveseat. In its original form it had one big bedroom and that's why it was named "Honeymoon." But one of the previous resort owners divided the bedroom into two small rooms, each big enough only for the beds. The worst part of this cabin was that it was lopsided and no one ever wanted to re-book it. As for the Wolf Den, I loved this little cabin. It looked a lot like Al Capone's cabin, which still stands as a little tourist destination in the Northwoods. Once we replaced the leaky roof, we thought it had many years of life left in it. But in order to move it, to build the big, three bedroom, two bathroom deluxe unit we had in mind, it would have cost $10,000 and the life of thirty trees. And while we could have recouped the money in rental fees in about three years, the trees would have been a permanent sacrifice—a sacrifice we didn't want to make. So, the Wolf Den bit the dust. By that time our full-grown wolf pups had outgrown the place, too. (But my brother's family is still disappointed in us for tearing down what was their favorite cabin.) The new cabin, which we named "The Marq" after the

Marquette Medical Systems stock we sold to build it, was instantly popular with the guests and we rented it for more than what we had rented both of the old cabins together.

Cabin Five, The Uncommon Loon, was the next to go. And it was replaced with a cabin so beautiful it can now be called our signature cabin. We named it after the original "The Big House" as a guilty tribute to all the trash we created by tearing down the old units. Much to my surprise and protests Cabin Two, Zeke's Lair, met its fate during the same winter we demolished number five. A crafty contractor insisted he could build a new cabin in its place for a reasonable price as long as he already had his crew on the property. Unfortunately it was already rented out at the rate for the old cabin and we didn't see the financial benefits of the replacement until the following summer. But it was a simple case of the old cabins looking too shabby next to the new ones. And guests were happy to rebook.

Each summer guests reserve the same cabins for corresponding weeks of the following summer. This is how we tend to book up a year in advance. We, however, don't require the non-refundable deposits until January in order to give them an out in case something comes up over the holidays (like a family wedding or a trip to Disneyland). Some people can't set their vacation schedules until after the first of the year and occasionally we have cancellations for this reason. This gives new people an in. And there are plenty of new people looking for a nice place in the Northwoods for a family vacation, especially since the number of small resorts decreases each year.

In the 1970s there were approximately seventeen resorts on Squaw Lake alone. Today there are two in operation, another for sale, and a bed-and-breakfast that according to some of its misplaced guests, closed during the summer of 2001 for a sort of sabbatical. Each week people stop by our office looking for accommodations for the following summer because owners of the resorts where they had been staying are selling off the cabins or "going condo." And while this is a good thing for our business, it also means we have seen an increase in the occupancy levels in our units. Nearly every week they're packed to maximum capacity and then host dinners for additional family members and friends from surrounding hotels and campgrounds, who weren't lucky enough to find resort accommodations at Sandy Point or another resort property. This translates to higher septic and trash bills as well as greater wear and tear on the cabins and a need for constant maintenance. Just when we think we've finished remodeling, another unit requires new carpeting, doors or bathroom fixtures. We're convinced that the cabins will always provide ongoing, expensive projects.

All in all our vision tweaked itself from the romantic idea of cozy log cabins in the woods into a business plan consisting of deluxe, log-sided homes. After seven years of living on love and making no money, we became determined to make this thing work. In one of the early years, we were faced with an IRS audit. The red flag waving in the face of the government was a Schedule C form. We didn't make a profit. So, we were subjected to the typical collection and presentation of records and receipts, as well as scrutinizing agent interviews and phone calls. We had to prove we weren't operating our business as a hobby, but rather as a legitimate business in start-up mode. We were successful in that regard. But during the hassle of the audit, where every question seemed like an accusation, our accountant insisted everything would be okay. He said that while anyone in this country is allowed to start up and operate a business, there was no law saying the business had to be profitable. So, like an aging person stretching the piece of paper to an arm's length in order to read the small print without reading glasses, we have finally made our way into the black and continue to have far-sighted vision.

The Job

When people tell me I'm living their dream life, I think they're lucky people with happy and fanciful dreams. Indeed, it's a romantic notion for a young couple to sell off their worldly possessions, quit their city jobs and move to the woods to live at their own version of Walden Pond. But operating a resort is a job like any job with its good, bad, easy, difficult, rewarding and challenging aspects. And owning a resort is like owning any business. Self-employed people may get to set their own hours and not answer to a boss, but those hours are always long and that boss called "self" can be very demanding.

In our mom-and-pop operation I, mom, took on fifty-percent of the responsibilities and Mike, pop, took on the other half. In short, I do laundry and talk on the phone and Mike fixes things. Naturally, however, there are other jobs that are a part of running a resort.

Lots of them.

Mike and I were lucky because the division of chores happened naturally. We each gravitated to the areas where we had some knowledge and ability, or to the jobs that seemed more suited to each of us. What we didn't know we tried to learn. This doesn't mean our jobs are cut and dried and neither of us wanders over into the other's territory. It is, in fact, essential that we each know how to do the other's jobs. I can't fix things like Mike, but I can sometimes get through a repair using tools I no longer refer to as "thing-a-ma-bobs" and "do-hickeys." I may wear a Wonderbra but I know the power of a Wonderbar. I also know the rule of "righty tighty and lefty lucy," and the difference between a phillips and flat-head screw driver. I learned to never use my hand as a hammer, and even though I still can't quite find a way to wear that hammer so it doesn't swing between my legs, I think I look pretty cool wearing a tool belt. What this means I'm not sure, but I do know that I have never, ever let my butt crack slip out of my Levis.

Mike, who always has his tools in place, can certainly answer the phone and take a reservation, but even after years of operation he still double-checks the rates with me. Usually when the resort line rings he either waits for me to answer it or suggests that I do. He's heard me give the speech a thousand times and is pretty good at mocking me: "After we run your card, we'll send you a res-er-va-tion con-fir-ma-tion . . ." But when it comes to reciting the speech in his own voice, he almost always leaves something out. And it's important stuff like the cancellation policy or that we *do* provide bed linens but *don't* provide towels. Even though we send all this information in writing with the confirmation, people either don't read it or they forget and need to be reminded. If one more person comes to my door and tells me I forgot to equip the cabins with towels, I'm going to roll up a wet one and swat him in the legs.

Thank goodness each of us has specific areas of expertise, and for the sake of Sandy Point's success and reputation we concentrate on doing the jobs more tailored to our personalities.

For example, Mike doesn't operate the computer program that keeps our bookkeeping in order and our checkbook balanced. It's appropriately called, M.Y.O.B., M for Managing, not Minding, Your Own Business. As for the paperwork, well, I won't let him touch it. Like any good office manager, I'm anal and organized. At least I *was* organized before I had children. But I'm resting on my laurels. And no matter how strong I think I might be, I simply cannot lift picnic tables or other furniture over my head and carry them from cabin to cabin when guests decide to rearrange. One time I watched Mike pick up a sofa, heave it over his head, and then transport it from one cabin to another in the snow. I walked behind him and marveled at his strength.

"I can't do that," I said out loud. "Wouldn't even try."

I'm Living Your Dream Life

I guess it's fair to say that I'm the brains and Mike's the brawn. The yin to his yang, I decide where the furniture should go and he gets it there.

Mike is the "super." He walks around with a big, jangling key ring and is on call twenty-four-hours a day tending to all the malfunctions. He relights pilot lights, replaces light bulbs, hits reset buttons on GFCI outlets when guests use all the appliances and their hair dryers at the same time. He plunges out toilets, snakes out septic systems, stops the drips and finds the leaks. He tracks, traps, and cleans up after decaying rodents, sprays for ants and is the best bat catcher any resort guest could ever hope to have in charge. Mike fixes the soda machine when it refuses to provide change and always locates the cue ball for the pool table, which is either stuck in the bowels of the table or thrown into the recreation house garbage can by some rambunctious five-year-old. He's also been known to get that same five-year-old off of the pool table and back onto the floor, and clean up after him when he's poured soda into the pockets or used the cue stick to poke out a few panes of glass in the French doors.

People break things. Mike fixes them.

People also create a lot of trash. Each year we refine our recycling policy in order to make the sickening job of sorting garbage a little easier. Wisconsin has fairly strict recycling rules and the local dump won't take unsorted trash. We are avid recyclers and are always amazed and disgusted when guests refuse to separate the aluminum, glass and plastic. In our first years of operation the guests from Illinois (Chicago in particular), where there was no recycling system in place, were the worst. At check-in time I went over the policy until their eyes rolled into the backs of their heads, and also had instructions in a framed wall-hanging in each cabin. I did my best to help educate the guests, just to save Mike from his most dreaded chore. They've gotten better, thank goodness, especially since Chicago instigated a "Blue Bag" recycling system. Nevertheless, no recycling plan can get Mike out of the chore of emptying the reeking bins of the fish-cleaning house each week. I'm afraid no one has any use for fish guts.

Mike is also chief groundskeeper and I am his assistant. In late April—or when the snow finally melts for the season—it's time to clear about ten acres of property around the cabins of last fall's soggy, decomposed leaves. That's the ironic thing about all those beautiful leaves I described earlier. Every year they put on their show and then drop to the ground by the millions to be cleaned up like so much garbage.

In the Northwoods we have four seasons in name only. In reality there are only two: Winter and Fourth of July. The ABC book I read to my kids called *Antler, Bear, Canoe*, uses the twenty-six letters of the alphabet to sum up the Northwoods seasons and approximately four of those letters are dedicated to summer. The rest are dedicated to cold weather chores and what we face each year. Take the letter J, for example. It stands for junk.

"...When the snow melts, all the junk shows up. Sometimes we find treasures we had forgotten about, but always there are things to load up and take to the dump." Usually the only treasures we find are lost basketballs and golf discs, and it's little reward for the relentless raking.

Whenever it's time to clear the leaves, it feels like we just finished that chore. The first year we used rakes until our hands were covered with blisters. We worked on a new section of property each day, amassing piles until they were three-feet high, and then transferred them to a giant blue tarp and lifted the load to the back of a pickup truck to then haul to a dumpsite deep into the property. It didn't take another season of that laborious chore before we added a push blower and a backpack leaf blower to the equipment shed. It was well worth the investment. When we can find outside help to assist in this job, we always make room for it in the budget.

But the leaves don't just fall on the ground. They also fall into the lake. And the price we pay to be home to one of the best sandy beaches in the Northwoods is a whole lot of summer-long maintenance.

Sandy Point rests on the north shore of Squaw Lake. With the prevailing winds from the south it means that almost every leaf, stick, feather or sardine can, t-shirt, cigarette package, bottle rocket, fishing lure, dead fish and even the occasional driver's license eventually ends up on our shore. And while it also means the beautiful sugar sand washes ashore daily— giving us a good reason for the name Sandy Point—it's a bitch to clean up after a long frozen winter.

A tool has yet to be invented to make clearing a shoreline in spring an easy job. Every year, witnesses to our shoreline-clearing job say that there's got to be an easier way of getting it done. One person suggested we get a box-spring mattress, strip the fabric and use it to drag the leaves. Someone else suggested using the snowplow. But these things don't work. We've tried. So we continue to use a giant metal rake to make the piles, and then a smaller wire rake to get up the small stuff and smooth the sand. The leaves are black, thick and heavy, and they extend from the shore out about fifteen to twenty feet. We wade into the water and rake them back to the shore a small section at a time, then leave them on the beach to dry for a day or so to make for a lighter load before piling and loading them into the back of the truck. Mike starts by hauling out about ten full truckloads collected from just over five-hundred-feet of shoreline. The leaves are stashed in a low spot in the woods just off the beach. Some day we're going to have a huge dune where the leaves have decomposed and the sand has remained. In the next phase, he uses a wheelbarrow instead of the truck. Occasionally the results of a windy day during the summer may require the truck again, but once we get into late May and June the wheelbarrow does the job daily for the rest of the summer.

The beach at Sandy Point is one of the resort's nicest features. It's worth our time and effort to keep it clean and raked on a daily basis. One of the first things we do each morning in the summer is put away all the sand toys, clean up any garbage left behind and rearrange the furniture. This is my favorite time of day. While most vacationers take the opportunity to sleep in, or fry bacon for a big breakfast—there's always the aroma of bacon in the air around the cabins in the morning—I like to have the beach to myself. After putting away the toys and straightening everything for the new day, I sit in a swinging chair that's attached to two trees and stare out at the lake. I hear feint conversations of fisherman from almost a mile off the shore, and watch a bald eagle soar overhead looking for some breakfast to take back to the nest. The loons are out early as well, and by this time of morning they're through calling to each other in their eerie, tremulous voices and are busy diving and looking for fish.

If it's the middle of the week the grass stretching from the sand to the tree line is long, and filled with yellow, purple and orange wildflowers. Mike usually waits until the Saturday turnover to get out the riding lawn mower so guests aren't disturbed by the noise. He's got an army of lawn mowers. Since the riding mower can't be used everywhere, he uses push mowers and trimmers and all kinds of things requiring constant maintenance and gasoline. He received his lawn mower repair training at an early age and owes the skill to his father. One of Mike's chores as a boy was to keep the grass of their suburban home trimmed. Whenever he tried to get out of the task to go off and play with his friends, he broke the lawn mower. But that ploy didn't work on his wise old man. The usual response to "I can't mow the lawn because the mower's broken" was a stern: "Well then, bring it here and I'll show you how to fix it!"

I'm convinced Mike can fix anything, and this is a key requirement for the job of resort owner. When you take care of several dwellings, things are always in need of repair. And when you're dealing with rental units and a constant turnover of guests—some of whom are more high-maintenance than others—stuff just breaks. If we had to hire outside professional help each time something malfunctioned, we couldn't stay in business. For example, while we were out of town over the winter our caretaker was faced with a malfunctioning oven. One of our guests, who came to the resort for the purpose of making pies for her family, complained that the oven wasn't holding its temperature. If Mike had been there he would have replaced the thermal coupler, or whatever it took to get those pies baked correctly. But alas, he wasn't there and they had to call in a professional who showed up after the pie lady was gone. He fixed the oven, we think, and I was sent a bill for close to $200. We could have practically purchased a whole new oven for that amount.

Over the years we've managed to replace every mattress, stove/oven, refrigerator, coffee pot, toaster, and water heater and every cabin had a new roof before we tore it down. The time, expense and inconvenience of repair made the purchases and labor worth the investment. After updating the electrical systems of each cabin, we also added televisions, VCRs and microwave ovens, and only hope that they'll be treated well and last for several years.

I have a few job titles, ranging from cleaning lady to hostess to reservation manager. Frankly, I like to think of myself as Mother Superior—especially when I have to scold unruly teens making too much noise in the recreation cottage after quiet hours; but I get cut right down to size every Saturday when I start scrubbing the toilets.

My key jobs are: bed maker, sheet folder, kitchen organizer, bookkeeper and talking on the phone to prospective guests. I can even talk on the phone and fold sheets at the same time. In fact, I think I could win a sheet-folding contest—not only for speed, but also for four-corner neatness on fitted sheets in particular. One summer day when my now departed mother was visiting the resort, she marveled at my ability to fold sheets, as that's what I spent a good portion of each day doing. "You're so professional," she gushed.

"Oh mother," I sighed with what I thought was necessary sarcasm, "how proud you must be!" The truth is, my mother *was* proud. She was proud of me when I wrote the newspaper column and when I played well in sports. She was proud when I sang off-key and danced ungracefully on stage and honked on my clarinet or banged on the piano. She would have been proud of me no matter what I did. And this made me feel particularly good about my resort job of scrubbing toilets and making stainless steel fixtures sparkle. As long as I did what I chose to do well and with enthusiasm, Mom was proud.

And pride is an important issue. As a resort owner, you can't have too much of it. I may have a cleaning lady to clean my own home on a weekly basis, but come Saturday mornings at Sandy Point Resort *I* am the cleaning lady. And no one I hire is going to clean those cabins as well (or care as much about how clean they are) as I do. Here's an important fact that cannot be stressed enough: Guests want clean cabins. Just like one typo can wreck your credibility as a journalist, one poop-stain on a blanket can convince your guests that your cabins are nothing but germ and disease infested dwellings. And they'll be sure to tell everyone they know. It's a marketing fact that people who have good experiences with a business will usually tell one or two people about it. When people have bad experiences they tell ten. They'll even tell strangers.

In our first year of operation with five small cabins, Mike and I cleaned them all ourselves. When we added more cabins, we took on some cleaning help. But as good help is hard to find, ultimately we're back to cleaning everything ourselves. It's always like a marathon, where we breathlessly come up for air after making thirty-three beds, scrubbing eleven toilets and scouring eight kitchens in less than six hours on Saturdays; but we always make our deadline, and we're sure everything is clean.

Our units are known as "housekeeping units," which means they are ready when guests arrive but we don't go in on a daily basis and wash dishes, make beds and leave mints on the pillows. During the week, we're on property to make any necessary repairs or to answer questions. Since in the summer our cabins are rented only by the week from Saturday to Saturday, it's Saturday—or turnover day—that's the big workday for us.

Each Saturday I get up at sunrise and organize sheets for eighteen bedrooms and cleaning supplies for the kitchens and bathrooms. I park myself on the front porch and anxiously await the gift of a guest who departs before the 9:00 am check-out time and then pounce, to try and get a jump-start on the process. In the first year of operation each cabin was small and took only an hour or less to get turned over: beds stripped and remade, bathrooms cleaned and sterilized, kitchens thoroughly revamped, vacuuming, dusting, and any repairs were done in five hours. This gave Mike enough time to move to the grounds and me enough time to grab a bite to eat, shower off the cleaning lady scum and turn into the colorfully dressed, clean, lady hostess. From 3:30 until about 8:00 pm, I stay on duty greeting and checking-in guests. At this point, Saturday turns from cleaning day into payday.

When our resort grew to include two year-round units, each requiring a little over an hour to clean, and then grew again to include the unit we call Lakeview Lodge, with its four bedrooms, three bathrooms and two kitchens—and sometimes because of its fourteen inhabitants—it took us significantly longer to get ready for arriving guests. So, we thought it was time to hire some help. First we hired a teenage girl. She was adorable and always showed up. She wasn't the best cleaning lady in the world, but I devised ways to get her to double-check her work.

"For every hair I find stranded in the bathroom," I said, "I'm going to charge you a quarter." Except for maybe a poop-stain on a blanket, nothing is worse than a hair in the bathtub.

And the year after that, this same girl found a couple friends to join the staff. Their cleaning skills were even worse than her's and they didn't always show up. But they were cute and young, and had active social lives. I listened to their stories and lived vicariously through them as we cleaned and scrubbed. In the fall they went off to college, and were all well on their way to occupations far more important and prestigious than making beds and cleaning bathrooms.

The first job in cleaning a cabin is to clear the dirty sheets and get them to the laundry, which in our case consists of commercial size machines in the basement of our house. I use a golf cart to zip from cabin to cabin because time is of the essence. I drive the cart at top speed and often leave behind a trail of pillowcases in my wake.

Beds are made with hospital corners and quilts and pillows are positioned just right. I believe that bed making is a fine art. My Irish twin sister claims that when I was an adolescent and didn't make my bed because I was lazy I used to say, "I don't make my bed, because I don't know how." I've come a long way baby, because I now believe there shouldn't be the slightest hint that the bed had been slept in the night before—or ever, for that matter. The dimes won't bounce off the mattresses back into your hand, but the beds definitely beckon you to get in and get comfortable. I have two sets of sheets for each bed with a few sets stored for emergencies. One set is made into the bed; the other is stripped, promptly washed, and stored for the next week. Blankets and quilts or bedspreads are not changed each week, but always checked for reusability and periodically laundered and replaced. I check for stains. Stains are the enemy. And this is something I didn't expect: People bleed. A lot.

Obviously, as a woman I'm aware of what can occasionally happen to the sheets, but I didn't realize that among other things kids bleed from the mouth and stain the pillowcases. I don't know if their teeth are falling out or their chapped lips are cracking and bleeding or if people are just punching them in the face. But I do know they get lots of mosquito bites and they scratch them in their sleep until the blood flows and stains the sheets.

And speaking of mosquitoes, they like to hang out in bathrooms. I don't think a week has gone by where I haven't had to clean up the remains of a dead mosquito squashed on the bathroom wall with a blood red comet tail of its last supper streaking behind the corpse.

Some kids eat in bed, too. I thought it was a universal parental rule to forbid eating anywhere other than at the table. But at the resort people are on vacation, and rules tend to take a break as well. Spilled milk and orange juice regularly stain blankets. And let's not forget to mention that kids in potty training wet the bed every week. If it happens early in the week, I might get a smelly, wet deposit on my front doorstep with the request for a new set of sheets and blankets. It's why I keep emergency sets of bedding on hand. The nice, kind mothers will spare me and launder the sheets themselves, either in the facilities we provide (only two of our units offer a washer and dryer) or at a Laundromat in town. Most of the kids, however, for some reason tend to wait until the last night to wet the bed, and the parents, in a hurry to pack up and meet the 9:00 am check-out deadline, "forget" to tell me about the accident.

Due to so many incidents of pee-soaked sheets (after having gotten my own children through that stage), I must admit I'm a little irregular with my sheet congeniality. Given the amount of work involved with laundry each week, I'm usually pretty resentful when I have to wash and hand out another set of sheets. If I like the guest or they're "regulars," I'm happy to oblige and just feel sorry for the kid and the parent that they have to deal with the mess at all. But if it happens to the same kid more than once in the week, or the parents don't apologize but simply drop off that soiled mess for me to deal with, or expect me to come and remake the bed, then I get a little, well, pissy. "We don't offer a sheet service," I say.

Regular bed-wetting makes it necessary to protect each mattress with a plastic bed-liner. And we keep plenty of these on hand, because for unknown reasons people take them off and throw them away. And these are nice liners, not the kind that make noise when you lie on top of them, but the kind with a zipper that cost a couple bucks each. Bed-wetting is also the reason to always double-check the mattress pads. Those unmistakable yellow rings show up all summer long even though a bed-wetting incident went unreported. And the stains don't always come out, no matter how you pretreat them. I run out of usable mattress pads every summer, and am thinking of dying them a RIT-flavored butterscotch or lemon yellow. Whoever decided that they all had to be white?

We also have on hand a large stash of extra cooking and eating utensils.

As our cabin's kitchens are fully equipped with plates, glasses, flatware and cookware, we find the supply in each cabin changes or dwindles a little bit each week. I don't know where all the forks and spoons go, but they go. Glasses break, dishes crack and chip. Cookware just wears out.

One week while I was cleaning one of our newer cabins, I couldn't find a single glass. I checked all the cabinets and drawers, looked in the bedrooms and bathroom and even checked the fireplace. Could they have been celebrating by throwing glasses into the fireplace? I couldn't believe they were stolen. They were cheap, silly little drinking glasses. This cabin in particular has developed a history of disappearing glasses. We finally realized that it was because of the shallow, porcelain kitchen sink, and now know that all kitchen sinks must be deep and stainless steel so glasses won't break so easily during washing. For that cabin, we invested in heavy-duty, sturdier drinking glasses and added rubber liners for the sinks.

Another problem with dishes and cookware is that they float from cabin to cabin. This happens because of groups. We typically have weeks where large families come for an annual reunion and they stay in several different cabins. One night they prepare a meal and eat at one place, the next night it's at another cabin. I try to keep my eye on where they eat the last night so when I go into one cabin on Saturday morning and find zero forks, I can guess where they've been stashed. Rearranging the cookware and cleaning out all the cabin booty from the refrigerators and cabinets takes a good half-hour each Saturday.

Cabin booty, which consists of condiments like ketchup, mustard, mayonnaise, and Miracle Whip (which we promptly throw away) have our personal household refrigerators well-supplied all summer long. The other items we never need to buy during the summer are Popsicles, charcoal and lighter fluid. We also get milk, orange juice, beer and frozen waffles. Sometimes people leave fresh fruit and vegetables, candles and flower arrangements. They forget their CDs and tapes in the cabin's boom boxes, their battery chargers and computer cables, and every week we find kids' toys and kids' clothes in and under the furniture.

Except for the food, which we know guests leave on purpose, everything we find goes into a storage box. Our policy is if they call, we send it. And depending on how heavy or valuable it is, we usually send it COD. If they don't call, it stays in the box. With the amount of stuff left behind each week we would need to hire a full-time cabin booty manager to keep track of who left what in which cabin, and then pack and ship it back to the rightful owners.

Recently, I was at my daughter's school sorting through the lost and found, trying to find a missing sweater. At first I thought it was just a small stash in the principal's office, but the secretary informed me there were six more giant bags located on the stage in the cafeteria filled with kids' coats, sweaters, shoes, lunch boxes, underpants (yes underpants) and other clothing items. There was enough material there to clothe a small town. Clearly, the lack of responsibility for personal items starts at an early age and continues throughout life.

The heaviest things I've had to return were a man's pair of ostrich-skin cowboy boots, and the most valuable was a laptop computer. The silliest thing was a kid's two-dollar ball. But some of the most important things I've sent year after year are little kids' favorite stuffed animals or a blankey, which I know from experience are vital to a family's peace of mind. What remains in a large box in our basement, sitting there like an island of misfit clothing, is a collection not as large as the one at school, but close. After deciding that Rudolph the Red Nosed Reindeer and Santa weren't going to show up on Christmas Eve and take all the items to homes in need, we periodically drop off the clothing at the tribal center on the nearby Indian Reservation.

My job as cleaning lady ends each Saturday after I take one last cruise through each of the cabins to do the final inspection. I add things like extra toilet paper or a trash can or oven liner, and power up the refrigerators. I then close and lock the doors to keep guests from moving into their cabins before registering and paying, and to keep out the dirty feet of strangers visiting the grounds.

One Saturday several years back I was on final inspection duty, when I entered one of our newer cabins. Immediately upon stepping inside, I heard the dull hum of the bathroom's exhaust fan and saw that the light was on as well.

"That's odd," I said out loud. I remembered turning off all the lights in that cabin just a few minutes earlier. So I walked into the bathroom, only to find the toilet paper roll unwound. The paper hung like a celebration streamer, and lo and behold, somebody had left a little gift in the toilet as well. I was outraged! Even if I hadn't just cleaned and sterilized that bathroom for the new guests, who were due to arrive within the hour, I couldn't believe someone just came in, took a dump and left it there to mock me. There's a public outhouse located closer to this cabin than any other, which someone had passed right by. And it's not a yucky outhouse. It's got the requisite moon carved into the door, is whitewashed, clean, offers toilet paper, and even has potpourri hanging on the wall in a heart-shaped container.

I flew out of the cabin to see if I could find the culprit. Whoever it was, he couldn't be far. There were a couple kids (who I knew well) on the disc golf course. They were regular players.

"Did you use the bathroom in that cabin?" I asked pointing back at the unit.

"No," they said in unison. I believed them, aware they knew better.

"But did you see anyone come out of that cabin just now?"

Again they said "No" in unison.

"Well, did you see anyone you didn't know?"

"Yes," said one boy. "There was a couple—a man and a woman—walking around. But they left."

I wanted to quickly grab my keys, jump in the truck and chase after them. To do what, I wasn't sure. Scold them for not flushing? Looking at my watch, however, it was too close to the deadline for arriving guests and I hadn't even eaten or showered yet. So, I just retrieved the cleaning supplies and sterilized the toilet again, and was sure to lock the door of the cabin behind me. I've been locking the doors ever since.

People wander onto the property all the time. Those who aren't staying with us are often shopping for accommodations for next year. Some drive in when they see the sign at the end of our lane and once they see us, act like they've been caught snooping and drive right back out. We refer to them as "drive-by shooters," and simply salute their taillights. Those who actually stop, park and get out of the car almost always prove to be the most delightful visitors. This is how we get the majority of our new business. I may spend a lot of time updating our website and answering e-mail and the phone, but once people see Sandy Point the place just sells itself.

Not everyone who stops is looking for accommodations, however. When people need help, they go to a place with a sign. One night when I was pregnant with my first daughter, the doorbell rang at about ten o'clock. That was a time when I could still stay awake until ten o'clock, and Mike and I had already finished our nightly game of Scrabble and he had gone to bed. We didn't have any guests at the resort and I didn't hear a car drive up, so I actually thought I might have imagined the doorbell. But an urgent pounding quickly followed.

"What is it?" I shouted towards the door. Holding the handle, I leaned over to the glass window next to the door and looked outside. Standing there was a man whose head was covered in blood. "Oh my God," I gasped, and opened the door.

"I was in a car accident," he said. "A deer jumped out in front of me and I ran the car off the road."

But often, they're looking for directions. I simply cannot believe how many lost people there are driving in the woods each summer. They have a vague idea of where they want to go, some even have addresses that make little sense and assume that since we have a sign hanging out on the road we're like the guys at the local gas station and will tell them where to go. I always do my best—but spend far too much time giving out advice. It happens on the phone, too. But those who call the toll free line aren't really lost. They're cheap. They call the number with no intention of booking a cabin with us.

"I see from your website that you're booked for the summer, but I'd like to know what you think of this other resort? They only rent by the week, too? What's with you people? What? A hotel? Well can you give me the name and numbers of some local hotels? And while you're at it, who do you recommend to use for boat rentals? And can you get me their numbers, too?"

We have a lot more outside traffic coming in since we started advertising the disc golf course and built the pro shop. A lot of my day is spent inside the shop, collecting four-dollar green fees and selling golf discs. When the shop was new to our operation, I got really excited when anyone bought something. In addition to golf discs and other things relating to the activity, we sell a lot of jewelry and decorative items. Adding a retail operation to the business allowed my job description to evolve even more. Now I have chores like "inventory" and more sales tax to compute and write up in monthly reports. Of course, I get to shop for that inventory in the off-season, and that job has proved to be pretty darn fun.

Any resort owner has to be prepared to answer a lot of questions about not only the resort, but also about the area. Each summer we come face-to-face with toads, snakes, butterflies, fish, and leeches for identification. Injured birds, squirrels, chipmunks, foxes and a menagerie of other critters are brought to us in boxes, with beseeching eyes asking for help. Bouquets of wildflowers are presented and questions like "what kind of pine tree is that?" constantly confront us. Qualified or not, we have become makeshift naturalists. I have a library of field guides which I use to identify birds, trees, flowers, reptiles and amphibians, and it amazes me how often I have to resort to these reference books when something unusual comes to the front door. When I can't find it in the books I go to the Internet, and have been known to deliver an information package to the kid who found the orange toad, as if his report was due in the morning. Remember, I was trained to dabble in any subject. During my first two years of college, I worked as a secretary and receptionist in the Zoology Department at Southern Illinois University. And while I didn't take any of the entomology, herpetology or ichthyology courses they offered, I typed the professor's books and presentation papers and their exams. I learned quite a bit about critters while working there.

Each week during the summer season we have what we call the "bug de jour" factor. For the most part, the annual infestation is predictable. The first bug to make the scene when the temperatures warm in May is the black fly. Perhaps better known as gnats, the three to five-day period where these tiny black bugs swarm are the worst days to be outside raking leaves or playing disc golf. Imagine Pig Pen, the Peanuts character, the dirty little boy who always had a gray cloud hovering around. That's what anyone standing outside looks like when the black flies are in season. Even if you bathe in the morning, the swarm will hover around your head while individual gnats go in for the bite. They love to nip at your skull. If raking leaves is on the agenda while the black flies are in season, it cannot be done without the use of a green-netted face shield. One year the black flies were late and coincided with our Memorial Day weekend disc golf tournament. I competed that year and found it nearly impossible to line up and concentrate on a putt, because I not only had black dots blinking out my vision like a strange case of macular degeneration, but I also had to keep swatting them away.

In May of 1998, we saw a new infestation of something known as the tent caterpillar. Like an inchworm about one inch in length, these multi-legged creatures give me the creeps just thinking about them. I've heard them called army worms, too. They have soft, yellowish bottoms and brown bodies with dark green and light blue stripes and are primarily found in large clusters climbing on trees. They crawl to the tops of the tall birch and poplar trees (apparently the delicacies of the worm world) to feast on the leaves. Then they lay their eggs and from the top branches spend the day digesting, while defecation falls to the ground like a soft rain. At night they spin webs from tree to tree so that come morning a white film covers the forest, and it looks like the haunted houses people set up at Halloween.

Their infestation lifecycle is said to be from three to five years. In the years 1999 and 2000 it was worse, and while we hoped for the three-year estimate to be correct, by the spring of 2001, tens of thousands of caterpillars ate away our forests. The trees were so bare it looked like winter. Caterpillars were everywhere. It was impossible to sit down on the benches of our disc golf course. Even if you cleared the bench, by the time you came back to it during the next round it was filled again. And if you talked real loud or screamed obscenities in their general direction, they raised the top halves of their bodies and wiggled, as if shaking their fists in protest. They dropped from the trees onto our heads and into our golf bags, and we knew our outer clothing was covered with poop. At their peak our asphalt driveway looked like a giant black, slithering snake, as the ground was completely carpeted. At first I walked as though on hot lava, tiptoeing and jumping from side to side to avoid squashing these things and soiling the bottom of my shoes. But after several weeks I got bolder. I walked across the driveway taking a new route with each trip, stomping like a kid walking through puddles.

I was not the only one to declare war on the caterpillars. By mid-June, it was rumored that the Wisconsin Department of Natural Resources released something like forty million big black flies, bigger than a housefly, to combat the caterpillars. I called them "Super Flies" and half-expected them to appear in bright red capes. But the DNR simply called these flies non-biting and non-invasive, and they were meant to eat the larvae of the tent caterpillars. (It was reported that the only other thing that would destroy the larvae and save us from another infestation the following spring was if the winter temperature reached forty-below.) And while these flies may have been non-biting, they could hardly be called non-invasive.

One day I took my daughters to the beach to swim and brought my laptop with me to take care of a little business. Within five minutes, I had to change my vantage point three times. I started on the chair-swing in the shade, and then moved to a chair in the sun. Each place I moved, flies still covered me. So, I went out on the dock thinking the slight breeze out there might keep the flies away from me. It was a little better, but not much. I was never bit by a super fly, but personally I felt very invaded. They kept landing on my keyboard and I thought they might start typing in self-defense. At one point there were five crawling on the screen and keyboard, exploring the computer like it might have been a meal. No wonder we had the beach to ourselves that day. Even though it was a beautifully warm day and the lake was calm, all the guests were either hunkered down inside their cabins or shopping in town, where the trees weren't as plentiful. But the infestation hit town as well. Each time I took my daughters there for piano or gymnastics lessons, caterpillars dropped from the sky and coated the windshield of my car.

The next flying insect to make an appearance is the Mayfly. Mayflies in Dutch are called "One Day Flies." In their short life, the adults don't even eat or drink. They mate, the female drops her eggs in the water and they die. Mayflies are primitive insects that have been flying around for millions of years. And while they might come in May in places south of us, in the Northwoods they make their presence known in June. What's significant about the Mayflies is that there are millions and, as any fly fisherman can tell you, they are a delicacy for the fish. When they land on the water, and they're light enough to sit on top of the waves, the fish snap them up like lures. In addition to a short lifespan, their infestation only lasts three or four days. But during this little stint the fishermen complain that the fish aren't biting. (There are always fishermen complaining that the fish aren't biting, but that's the excuse we use during the Mayfly season.) Also, it's not the time to leave your front porch light on at night. As the Mayflies are attracted to light, when you open the door in the morning the screens and the house siding around the light are covered like wallpaper. Since many are exhausted from their mating ritual and ready to die or are already dead, you have to either pluck their sticky bodies off the house or get a whiskbroom to do the job.

By the end of June, and into July and early August it's mosquito time. You may have seen it on a t-shirt or a post card, but there are many who consider the mosquito to be the Wisconsin state bird. Yes, they're big, and depending upon the spring rainfall, there can a lot of them. When it comes to mosquitoes, my job as a resort owner is to simply advise visitors on what type of repellant to use. Because if you plan to be outside anytime after 4:00 pm, you had better wear protection or face the consequences of being a Northwoods meal.

"Skin So Soft may smell good and make you feel more comfortable using it on your children, but trust me the mosquitoes laugh at that stuff," I say. "Invest in deet. It's the only thing that works."

Summer after summer I receive disapproving frowns from other parents or guests who are in the medical fields, warning me that the chemicals aren't good for us. But I've made my choice. I feel they might change their minds if they saw their daughters' skinny little legs and arms covered with itchy red welts they insist on scratching until blood flows down their limbs, running like a melting Popsicle.

Other flying critters include the dragonflies, which are bigger than Mayflies and buzz around all day like miniature helicopters. We also have a huge population of bats that come out after dark and swoop and dip in search of mosquitoes. Except for when they find their way into our house and cabins and freak out the guests, we love the bats.

Bats can work their way into buildings through the tiniest holes. Our house happens to be one of their favorite nesting sites and a summer hasn't gone by that we haven't had to deal with at least one bat in our house. Mike is particularly good at trapping them. While I hide under the sheets, peeking out only to watch my husband in action, he keeps a fishing net next to his bed as if it were a weapon that he might keep on standby to fend off a prowler. When the case of an intruding bat wakes us with the sound of its flapping wings and high-pitched squeal, he jumps up, grabs his net and immediately switches on all the lights.

"Darn," he yells, missing. "It's a fast little bugger." And then after a couple more attempts I hear, "Gotcha!" He then takes the net outside and releases the bat to eat up more of the dreaded mosquitoes.

One night several years back when we still had all the original cabins, cabins that were definitely bat infested, we heard a bloodcurdling scream in the middle of the night. It came from one of the cabins, and was so loud it woke us both. We looked at each other and said simultaneously, "bat." Sure enough, one of the city boys staying in The Wolf Den who was up in the Northwoods for the first time to fish, encountered a bat, he must have thought Dracula had come to suck his blood.

When I was little I heard that bats not only carry rabies and like to bite your neck, but they also like to build nests in your hair. And while vampire bats do not exist in North America, only an extremely small percentage of bats carry rabies. The bat accounts for one-fourth of the mammals on this planet and are the only mammal that can truly fly. I don't know anything about them building nests in little girl's heads, but I suppose it's probably my job to find out.

There are a lot of things I'm still learning about my job as a resort owner and operator. Each day brings a whole new host of questions, critters, pleasures and problems. Most of the questions from the guests we've heard before, but some are as unpredictable as the Wisconsin weather, and that's what keeps it interesting and challenging.

Most people I meet think cleaning the cabins and dealing with the pressure of a full-turnover Saturday is the hardest part about my job. One of my neighbors in Tucson, where we now spend our winters, actually seemed horrified by the idea of me being on the cleaning staff. "You don't actually get in there and scrub the toilets do you?"

"Of course I do," I said. "I'm not above that."

Cleaning is the easiest thing I do at the resort. Why? Because it's predictable. A toilet is a toilet is a toilet. You clean it and it doesn't talk back to you. When cleaning a cabin, you pretty much know what to expect. It starts out dirty and it ends up clean. There's a real sense of accomplishment with the task, and I find each Saturday when I close and lock the door before the next guests are due to arrive, I'm very proud of my work.

Mike and I are both proud of the work we've done and continue to do at Sandy Point Resort.

Frequently Asked Questions

One summer day when our daughter Willow was still a baby, I was at the beach with her. It was a Sunday afternoon, a time when I try to take a break each week to enjoy the property and mingle with the new guests. At the beach was a woman who was here for the first time. I think, in fact, she was in Wisconsin for the first time, up from the suburbs of somewhere. It was a warm day and most of us were dressed in bathing suits and playing with our kids in the sand and the water. She, on the other hand, wore long pants and a jacket and sat in the shade while her kids played.

At one point her young son began fiddling with something on his ankle that looked like a small leaf. "Hey mommy," he called, "look at this wormy-type thing on me. I can't get it off."

"Oh my God!" the woman yelled. "It's a LEECH!"

She rushed past me toward her son and scooped him into her arms like she was saving him from a shark. Her face was colored with terror. "What should I do?" she beseeched me.

"It's no big deal," I said. "I've got the salt right here."

I grabbed a salt shaker, which I keep handy by the boat house to sprinkle on anyone who gets a leech (which happens two or three times per summer) and poured salt onto the little wormy-type thing. Usually, it's a great show for the kids as the leech immediately shrivels up and falls off. Such was the case with this boy's leech, and he was thrilled about the whole experience.

But it was not the case for Mrs. Long Pants.

"You didn't TELL me this lake had leeches!" she cried.

What I wanted to say was, "You didn't ask." But I didn't. I told her that it was a live, fresh-water inland lake, and it was natural for it to have leeches.

"Well every other resort owner I spoke with said their lakes didn't have leeches," she said like a sassy child.

"Ma'am," I said calmly. "My guess is they either don't know the truth about fresh water lakes or they were lying." What I really believed was that SHE was lying. If she had asked "every other resort owner" about leeches, why didn't she ask me? Especially after she decided to come to our resort?

I'm a huge proponent of guests asking questions. I practically beg prospective guests to ask me questions about the resort and the surrounding area. "Once you get your reservation confirmation and list of guidelines in the mail, please don't hesitate to call our toll free line and ask any questions you might have." I repeat this statement word for word as though someone hits my control/copy button and out it comes each time I make a reservation. "I'm the owner of the resort and can answer any questions you might have, except for what the weather's going to be like."

"And what *will* the weather be like?" they inevitably ask.

My standard answer is, "Bring your sweatshirt. Bring your swimsuit."

I have learned not to predict the weather or quote the forecast. They used to be called weathermen, but now they're called meteorologists and they have a pretty difficult task in forecasting the changeable and unpredictable Wisconsin weather. Unfortunately, the reports I hear on the one local television station that regularly comes in clearly are usually wrong. If I then repeat the forecast to a concerned guest, then *I'm* wrong. I've actually had people blame me for the weather. Some people must think I've got a weather related remote under my front counter that I use to control the temperature like some evil villain in a Batman comic.

Here's a question I've heard more than once; "Why is it your weather is always rotten only when *we* come to your resort?" The frequency of this question has caused me to incorporate into our cancellation policy the statement that we don't give refunds due to weather conditions.

What follows are some of our all-time favorite questions and some of the other questions we hear week after week, year after year.

"Are there bugs up there?"

"Do you have air conditioning or should I bring my own unit?"

"Will my allergies bother me while I'm there?"

"What lake are you on?"

"Do you have a sandy beach?

"How far are your cabins from the water?'

"How far are you from town?"

"Are there phones in your cabins?"

"How far apart are the cabins?"

"Where's the nearest grocery store?"

"Do you have a pool?"

"Are your cabins heated?"

"Do your cabins have televisions, because I really can't stand to miss an episode of 'Regis and Kathie Lee.' "

"Should we bring our bikes?"

"Do you supply charcoal?"

"Do you take VISA?"

"Do you take cash?"

"Will you cash my check?"

"Where can I plug in my modem?"

"Can you send a fax for me?"

"May we have more coffee filters?"

"Do your cabins have fireplaces?"

"Where can we find firewood?"

"Do you sell bug spray?"

"Where's the ice machine?"

"Will you mail my letters?"

"How many acres do you have?"

"How'd you end up way out here?"

"Has this resort been in your family for generations?"

"Why are you called Sandy Point?"

"What kind of toilet paper do you supply? My husband needs a special brand."

"Do you have a better measuring cup than the one that's in the cabin? I need a perfect measurement in order to make pancakes for the kids."

"My mom is hot and the fan you gave us isn't enough. Can you bring us two more fans?"

"Can you wake me up at 4:30 am so I can meet the fishing guide?"

"I've locked myself out of the cabin again. Can I have another spare key?"

"How's the fishing?"

"What do you mean there are fish in this lake? I don't swim where there's fish."

"Are you sure there are fish in this lake? Because I'm sure not catching any."

"What kind of toad is this?"

"May I have another trash bag?"

"Can you baby-sit our kids while we go out to dinner?"

"How do I get to the boat ramp?"

"Why is the lake water brown?"

"Do you know anything about outboard motors?"

"Where should I park my trailer?"

"Can you back in my trailer for me?"

"Where can I rent a jet ski?"

"A snowmobile?"

"Is this snake poisonous?"

"What do I do if I run into a bear in the woods?"

"Do you have a volleyball?"

"We really need some extra time to get packed in the morning. Can we extend our check-out time until noon?"

"If it's a nice day on check-out day, can we stay and use the beach?"

I'm Living Your Dream Life

"Where should I dock my boat?"

"What do you mean I got in on a cancellation? I should have the right of first refusal next year."

"We know your dog policy requires preregistration and we see that you've got two dogs on the property already, but is it okay that we brought our dog anyway . . . and our bird?"

"Your policy says you don't allow cats. Why are you prejudiced against cats?"

"Can we leave our dog alone in the cabin all day if we put it in a kennel?"

"Where's the discount golf course?"

"How do you work the VCR?"

"Do your cabins have DVD players?"

"How do I get the cue ball out of the pool table?"

"Are we supposed to take the wax bag out of the cereal box before we recycle it?"

"Where should I park?"

"May I have an extra key for my relatives who are coming on Tuesday?"

"Can you give me change for the soda machine?"

"How do you work the pay phone?"

"Can you get my motor started?"

"Since it's just my wife and I in a three bedroom unit, can we get a discount?"

From the kids: "What can I buy for a dollar?"

"What kind of golf disc do you recommend for a beginner?"

"Where can I fill my water bottle?"

"Will you make a fire for me?"

"Will you plunge my toilet?"

"Can I get more gas for my motor?"

"Where can I plug in my battery charger for my trolling motor?"

"Can you tune in The Game on the TV at the Recreation Cottage?"

"Do you sell beer here?"

"Do all your cabins smell like this?"

"If we leave on Friday night instead of Saturday morning, can we get a discount?"

"What movies do you recommend for kids?"

"Can I drive my truck down to the beach?"

"Can I see your house?"

"What do I owe you for the broken glasses?"

"The coffee pot?"

"The microwave plate?"

"Will you take me water-skiing?"

"Where should we go to eat?"

"Can we use your golf cart?"

"When's the power coming back on?"

"Do you sell fishing licenses?"

"Will you carry my motor down to the lake for me?"

"What time does the water-ski show start in town?"

"Can I do a load of laundry at your house?"

"May I borrow your ax?"

"Your compressor?"

"Your battery charger?"

"Your truck?"

"Your jerry cans?"

"A screwdriver?"

"Do you want me to fix that squeak in your door?"

"What do you mean you don't sell bait?"

"Will you play disc golf with me?"

"What score do you usually shoot on this course?"

"Where are the paddles for the canoe?"

"Can I get some ping pong paddles?"

I'm Living Your Dream Life

"What stations can we get on the television?"

"When are you guys going to get individual satellite dishes for the cabins?"

"Can I rent your pontoon boat?"

"Which way is north?"

"How far away is the casino?"

"Is there a restaurant on the lake?"

"Why don't you have a bar here?"

"Where's the first tee?"

"How long have you owned this resort?"

"What did you do before you were resort owners?"

"How old are you guys, anyway?"

"What do you do in the off-season?"

"Do you work outside the home?"

Pause. Even though I mentioned it earlier, I've got to elaborate on that last question, "Do you work outside the home?" The first time I heard this question I thought it was pretty funny. My response was automatic. "You mean do I have another job besides running this business and taking care of my children?" I asked. Immediately, the woman who asked dropped her head and realized I thought her question was silly. The second time I gave the same response, the girl didn't get it at all.

"Yeah," she said. "Like do you have a job in town?"

"Where is the nearest church?" (I don't even ask anymore, because I know they're looking for a Catholic church. Only Catholics go to church while on vacation.)

"If I pay you in cash, can you take off the sales tax?"

"My baby feels hot. Can I borrow a thermometer?"

"Did you home-birth your children or is there a hospital nearby?"

"What do you do with your children during the day?"

"What do you mean your children are up at the house asleep? What if there's a fire?"

"These pillows aren't comfortable. Can we have new ones?"

"There's a white spot on these navy blue sheets that looks like detergent. Can we get a new set?"

"We're afraid of storms. Can we stay in your basement if it starts thundering?"

"We don't think any of your individual cabins are large enough for our group. Couldn't we just rent your house instead?"

"We want to read the latest Harry Potter book to our kids while here and couldn't find it in any of our local bookstores. Do you think you can order it for us from Amazon.com and have it sent overnight?"

(I had to explain to this guest that the whole world was looking for a copy of the latest Harry Potter book and that furthermore, there's practically no such thing as overnight delivery in or out of the Northwoods).

"My cell phone doesn't work here. Can I use yours?"

(I had to explain to this guest that nobody's cell phone works from our property).

"I flipped my truck about a mile down the road when I swerved to avoid a deer. Can you call me an ambulance?"

"We think we used to own this resort. Can you look at these photos and tell us if it's the right place?"

"I read through your rates and did the math. How do you guys manage a living at this business?"

"I know it's after office hours, but we'd really like to get another video. Can you open the shop?"

"Since they came into the world together, do our twins count as one person or two?"

"My kids were jumping on the bed and they broke through the springs. Can you come and fix it?"

"We're having a party at our cabin tonight. It's okay that all of our guests don't come and sign in, isn't it?"

"Do you have a towel service? Because if I have to use the same towel more than once I'll go bonkers." (I swear she used the word, "bonkers.")

"We know we're early, but we have ice cream melting in the car. Can we just get into the cabin to put it away?"

"Oh, the fridge isn't turned on yet? Can we store our food in your refrigerator?"

"Do you have a public restroom?"

"Oh, my wife won't use an outhouse. Couldn't she just use the bathroom in your house?"

"Do you have any openings for next summer?"

"What is disc golf anyway?"

"What is your philosophy in charging a green fee for your golf course?"

I should explain that most disc golf courses are located in public parks where there is no green fee, and this is what disc golfers expect. The way we address this frequently asked question is to point out that the public parks have city recreational departments who pay for the equipment, or have it donated by local Lion's or Rotary Clubs and pay for all the maintenance. Since our course is on private property where we pay the taxes and maintain the grounds, and purchased all the baskets and tee signs, our "philosophy" is that we're trying to get the people who use the course to help us pay for the expense.

"We're looking for property to buy. Do you know of anything for sale around here?"

And finally, each summer we hear this question two or three times from a variety of passing strangers, "We're looking for the so-and-so house, which is somewhere on Squaw Lake. We don't have an address or a phone number, but do you know them?" Sometimes we do know them, most times we don't. There are only a few year-round residents on the lake, and we explain that since we don't get out much during the summer, if our neighbors haven't stopped by to introduce themselves or play a round of disc golf, chances are we don't know them. We always pull out a local phone book and offer the use of our telephone to these lost souls. Sometimes we end up making a new friend from this simple act of hospitality. And they might even end up booking a cabin in the future, only to show up and ask us at least one of the above questions.

Meet the Neighbors

There's a paradox about modern living regarding neighbors and our need for each other in a community. City neighbors (where everyone lives right on top of everyone else) often don't even know each other's names. While country neighbors where homes are a farm apart, know the names and details of every family member. Common lore suggests that country neighbors need each other more to do things like raise barns and arrange marriages. City neighbors, tired of dealing with the noise all day, just want home to be a quiet place. They come home from work, drive into their garages, close the doors behind them with a remote, and that's it. At least this seemed to be the case in California. It was definitely the case for us in Oakland.

First of all, it was a hill community known as an urban forest. The same urban forest that burned down in a massive fire during October of 1991. The fire, even though it stopped about a mile from our street, did provide a temporary stage for a sort of neighborhood block party, as we all packed our possessions and commiserated in the high drama. But it was a short-lived social situation. The house to the west was below us and the house to the east was above us. And the massive eucalyptus and pine trees between us were so tall we couldn't see into each other's yards. We'd occasionally catch glimpses of each other as we backed our cars out of the driveway and looked homeward to see that our automatic garage doors were working, but we never socialized, and might not even recognize one another only a block away.

When we moved to the country and surrounded ourselves with forty acres of dense forest, not only could we not see the nearest neighbors, we weren't sure we had any. Town was some fifteen miles away down a narrow stretch of state highway; yet, it took us about the same amount of time to get to the nearest grocery store in our new setting as it did in the old. Why? No traffic. No stop lights. Without a doubt, we had moved to the sticks.

But there were indeed neighbors. And some of them knew a lot about us before we arrived. In fact, the first neighbor we met wandered over to our front porch one day before the snow melted.

"I hear you kids come from California," he said introducing himself. "And I know someone who went to your high school prom with one of your college roommates."

"Is that right?" I asked with a dropped jaw.

His story was true. He knew where I was from and about some of the people with whom I grew up. I wondered if a flyer had gone out about us with personal profiles, much like the ones we received from realtors in the neighborhood where I grew up. "Ed and Joan are from Chicago and have three children, ages eight, twelve and sixteen . . ."

A profile for Mike and me might have said something like, "Married for three years, this young couple left the big city and California dream behind for a simpler life in the Northwoods." (And apparently it also included a list of my college roommates and their dates.)

This particular neighbor might have been in property management or something, because he talked a lot about bad tenants. I wasn't sure if he was doing that for our benefit to warn us as new resort owners, or was simply rambling on about his own experience. He also knew a lot about the property we had just purchased.

"You say in your resort literature that you've got forty acres, but really it's more like thirty-nine. This here road cuts right through a big portion of your land on an easement, and part of your property juts right into the lake."

One night shortly after we moved in, a group of people from around the lake invited us to dinner to sort of introduce us to the neighborhood. We all drove in separate cars out west to the Moose Jaw Lodge and pigged out at an all-you-can-eat buffet. It was Northwoods Friday night fish-fare at its finest—a cafeteria-style buffet with a full bar amidst knotty pine walls filled with dead stuffed game.

The cast of characters included two couples (who called themselves "year-rounders" on the lake) who were friendly, intelligent and the age of our parents; a lady who chain-smoked, barked when she spoke, and was more interested in our wolf pups than us; a man who might have been our age or twenty years older, it was hard to tell, and his father, who were introduced as the finest carpenters in the Northwoods; another single gentleman who was at least twenty—maybe even thirty years older than we, who was also retired; and then another friendly, exuberant couple who talked a lot about fishing.

The evening went very well. Everyone was nice to us and asked a lot of questions. We really felt like they had high hopes for our business venture and that they were ready to welcome us into the neighborhood. During dinner I couldn't help but wonder whether this was going to be our new social circle. It was just a little bit different from our Frisbee friends and the Deadhead crowd.

Our neighbors may not have come over to throw golf discs or listen to music, but they were full of information. And we were usually glad to see anyone who dropped by. As new resort owners in the area, we needed all the information we could get.

"I see you got a problem with bats," said a passing neighbor one day while brushing aside some guano—or bat poop—with his foot from the front porch of our house.

"Is that what that stuff is?"

"Oh yes indeedy. They probably hang from the rafters during the day and then come out to eat up all the mosquitoes at night. Those little critters can eat ten thousand mosquitoes a night, you know. You oughta make a bat home for 'em. I make 'em. I made a pattern. Or you can go out and spend thirty bucks on one. But you should look into it."

Whenever we ran into our neighbors on the nearby roads, they had all kinds of advice. They had suggestions about what to do with the beach, how to handle the trash, what kind of dock we should buy, what kind of exercise we should get, the types of people we should associate with . . . The types of people we should associate with became a pretty big issue. As friendly and nice as everyone was, it was hard for us to fit in. The truth is we didn't have much—if anything—in common with the majority of our neighbors and we didn't have time to explore opportunities where we might feel more comfortable. Luckily, Mike and I were busy learning the resort business and getting the place in shape for our debut season. So, we relied on the company of each other during the day.

As the years passed, however, we made friends through an area softball league and then met some fun couples through a sand volleyball league. We also met people through our kids' sports program and the Chamber of Commerce, and ultimately, became friendly with a wonderful family who owned a resort just eight miles away. Indeed there are plenty of folks in the Northwoods with whom we've formed friendships, and we became socially content.

At one point, however, a large number of our neighbors decided they didn't want to be friends with us.

During our first season a group who was somehow related to residents in town, the sister-in-law of a daughter-in-law or something like that, stayed as guests at our resort. They were a group we inherited from the previous owners and they stuck out in my mind because they were late with their deposits. But three out of four eventually turned in their deposits and showed up for their scheduled week. They became our first experience with destructive tenants. It turned out this was the very group who made the previous owners want to get out of the business.

"We were going to buy this place," said one of the men to me one day while I was pulling weeds from the flower garden. "We've been coming here for a few years and it feels like ours."

I highly doubt they treated their own property the way they treated ours. They were loud and up late every night with what must have been ghost stories around the campfire, because kids screamed until midnight as if they'd heard eighteen versions of "the man with the golden arm." During that week so many things broke or were damaged that we saw more wear and tear on the equipment than we had seen all summer. One family who was staying in another cabin and not related to them left early because of them.

"We came here to relax but it's too loud. I'd rather go back to work," said the man.

Until that week, with only a few exceptions, we had had very good luck with the guests. Most of them were friendly and just happy to be on vacation. They were respectful of the property, complimentary of the changes and wanted to come back. We were happy to book cabins for them during the weeks they wanted, and flattered they wanted to return. Some wanted the same weeks and some wanted different weeks. Many wanted to try out different cabins. We decided to allow reservations on a first-come, first-served basis, giving priority to the guests who we believed treated the property well. We felt the need to develop our own client list, using our own experience as a reference.

On Saturday morning at departure time, the loud guests came to inform us that they'd be renting the same cabins again next year. And this is where we ran into trouble. I remember exactly what they said. "Do we need to even tell you that we'll be coming back next year?"

"Well, yes," I said. "We need to talk about that."

We had already rented out two of their cabins for the same week next year for a group that was coming in for a wedding. When we took the reservation back in June, we didn't realize that our future guests would dictate their "rights" to us.

"But this shouldn't be a problem," I said looking at their long, disappointed expressions, "because we're building two new cabins over the winter and they're going to be much nicer. You can have those if you want them."

"You rented out *our* cabins?" they asked incredulously. "How could you do that without asking us first?"

"Yes," said another. "You should have asked us first."

"I'm afraid we're still figuring out how we want to run this business," I said. "We inherited quite a few guests from the previous owners, but we have some guests of our own and you're just going to have to try to understand that as new owners we have new policies and we're really not sure how we feel about renting to big groups. But if you want me to hold the new cabins, I'd be more than happy to do so."

They were anything but happy. They stormed out of the office as though I had just shown them a sawed-off rifle and told them to get the hell off my land. A week later we received a long, scathing letter, telling us we didn't know anything about being in the resort business, and that we lied to them about renting out their cabins. It was filled with all kinds of judgments and insults, and also implied that our actions were going to come back to haunt us because they were going to report us to their friends in town. "It's going to cause you trouble with your neighbors," the letter promised.

"Why did you kick out our people?" asked their friend, who we considered a friend as well.

We explained that it was their choice not to come back. And that was the end of it. Or so we thought.

The season ended and while we strapped on our tool belts and busied ourselves with the construction of the new cabins, we didn't see much of the neighbors. All the summer residents went home and the year-rounders went into their annual hibernation mode. There were no more dinners or visits filled with advice. Occasionally we saw someone on the road during early morning hikes or driving by while we checked the mail, but only a wave was exchanged.

I'm Living Your Dream Life

Another summer passed, and week after week was filled with wonderful guests. We were very pleased with ourselves for pulling off another season and running the business on our terms. We weren't no rookies no more.

Late into the fall of 1994, as I grew large with my first pregnancy, we spent the winter mornings cross-country skiing on both our land and the neighboring properties. It was a quiet and uneventful winter until one day the phone rang. And even though he didn't identify himself, I recognized the voice of a man I had met several times.

"Say there," he said. "The house next to you is for sale. I'm looking at it in the paper."

"It is?" I asked. "That's news to me."

"Well, I think you should buy it."

"Don't you want to buy it?" I asked.

"I need another house like I need a hole in the head," he said. "Besides, I don't buy things from real estate agents. Maybe you guys could move in there and give yourselves a little privacy from the resort."

Without question, we wanted to buy that house. I had never been inside, but it was big and beautiful, sat on five acres and had over two hundred feet of shoreline attached to the three-hundred-feet we already owned. The retired couple living there at the time was very quiet. They had no dock and never used the lake. But in back they had a prolific flower, vegetable and fruit garden, and often asked me to come over to gather and take home some homegrown delights. The gentleman wasn't in good health and spent a lot of time tethered to an oxygen tank. They felt they needed to get a smaller place in town to be closer to the clinic.

When Mike and I first toured the house we knew immediately that it wasn't a place we'd move into, since it wasn't as large or as nice as our current home. But there was no doubt that it would make a fantastic rental unit. If updated and priced right, we thought it would pay for itself in under five years. This property, or what would soon become known as

Lakeview Lodge, was just a smart investment.

Our next-door neighbors were delighted to sell us their house. Negotiations went smoothly and with no children of their own, they left behind or sold us several household items including two kitchen and bedroom sets, far too many lounge chairs, a toolshed full of tools, a garage with a John Deere tractor and a Dodge pickup truck, and a lifetime collection of matchbooks, rubber bands, books, salt and pepper shakers, old shoes, and costume jewelry, as well as wine-making supplies, a craps table, and bags full of things we're still sorting through years later.

During escrow, there was one snag. One of the contingencies was that we had to have the property rezoned. It, like most of the properties on the lake, was designated a single-family residential unit; however, in order to legally rent it out a week at a time like the rest of our cabins, we had to apply for a new zoning designation. To meet our goal, we had the choice of a multifamily residential or recreational zoning. And because the resort was already zoned recreational, we tried to annex it to the resort property with a recreational zoning. So, we filled out the application, paid the fee, and scheduled the town and county zoning hearings. We assumed that would be the end of it.

But that was far from the end of it.

In early March we received a phone call from another resort owner, a friend south of us on the lake. "Hey, did you guys know there's a petition going around the lake against you?" she asked. "I got it in the mail the other day and I think you should see it."

And then another friend called. "You guys have some people badmouthing you around the lake. They're calling you the Sandy Point Developers and saying you're going to clear-cut the land and build high-rises. They plan to fight you at the zoning hearings."

Our friend brought us a copy of the petition, which was sent to every member of the lake association except for us, of course. A property owner we had never met who, to our knowledge had never set foot on our property, drew it up. The petition was filled with scare tactics, informing our "Squaw Lake Neighbors" that we, the Sandy Point Developers, planned to destroy the ecological integrity of the lake and wipe out the peaceful surroundings with five new acres of recreational property. It prompted rumors around town about our plans, including things we intended to build that made us laugh out loud. High-rise condominiums. A campground. An airplane landing strip. An off-road vehicle track. It was a long and ridiculous list.

The petition further stated that there was no other recreational property on the lake and all the land that wasn't already zoned single-family residential, like forestry land, for example, should be rezoned to discourage any further clear-cutting, development, or harm to the lake.

Sandy Point Resort has a legitimate recreational zoning, and until the Lake Association president became aware of this when we showed him the paperwork, he was on the side of the petitioners. Some claimed the previous owner of the resort railroaded the recreational zoning through the approval process during the year he acted as president of the lake association. Our argument was that every zoning issue is a matter of public record, and no zoning changes take place without public hearings. If the previous owner rode on a rail car, he did it in full public view. It turned out that the board members were just mad at themselves for not paying attention, and with little more discussion took their names off the petition and ultimately supported our effort. But that didn't mean everyone backed down. Some of our neighbors, clearly those who had nothing better to do during the doldrums of late winter and early spring, decided they wanted to fight this battle all the way to city hall.

The first town hearing in the meeting room of the Lac du Flambeau Town Hall was well-attended by Squaw Lake property owners. Our baby was only a few weeks old at the time, and when I walked into the room one of the first persons I saw was someone whose name was still on the petition. I walked in the opposite direction and spent a good portion of the meeting standing at the back of the room. I tried to keep the baby quiet by pacing with her and nursing her. I didn't want her to become the center of attention when there were important business matters at hand. I had done most of my important work in advance, preparing numbers indicating what we anticipated to be the actual residence time in Lakeview Lodge. We insisted that using it as a rental facility for only fifteen weeks per year would have less impact on the environment than a single family living there fifty-two weeks per year. We provided statistics regarding occupancy rates, as well as personal watercraft and boat use by resort guests. We outlined the entire history of Sandy Point Resort, indicating that it had been a family-run operation on Squaw Lake for over sixty years. We presented our current plans to redecorate the house and add a dock, and swore we had no plans to build an off-road vehicle track, an R-V park or an airport landing strip.

"What I want to know is what's going to happen to their property when these kids go belly up in a coupla years?" blurted out a man with a thick Milwaukee accent. "Who's to say some big developer *won't* come in there and tear up all the land?" He was new to the area and we hadn't yet met him. I walked up the side of the room along the line of folding metal chairs, most filled, some empty, and I glared at him. Who was he calling a kid? What did he know about Mike and me and how dare he assume we'd go belly up?

The people fighting against our measure had never even bothered to ask us what our plans were. They started passing rumors and a petition without meeting us, without viewing the property and without considering any of the qualifications for the zoning permit itself. We did not want to build high-rise condos or an airplane landing strip. All we wanted was to rent out Lakeview Lodge on a week-to-week basis and to go about it legally. Everyone in that room knew there were plenty of people on the lake with properties they rented out for weeks at a time during the summer, without considering the zoning laws or paying the appropriate taxes.

"I'm the person who is going to be most affected by this because I own quite a lot of property around these parts and I don't want to see my retirement ruined," said one man. It was the introduction to his environmentalist speech. And then, I swear he said this, "Squaw Lake is a lake for old people to sit around and watch the sunset."

The following saying is published in the local newspaper *The Lakeland Times*, about once a year. "A developer is a person who wants to build a home on a lake. An environmentalist is a person who already owns a home on a lake." I think the reason it's printed each year is because a lot of people just don't get it. The same battles between the haves and the wants happen every year. Naturally everyone understands that we don't want growth to get so out of control that we lose all the trees, pollute the lakes and destroy the reason we came here in the first place. But it's become easy to lose focus as the fearful crowd no longer fights growth, but instead fights change. I'd like to know when we became such a benevolent society full of hypocrites. We want all kinds of services, but we don't want to pay taxes. We say we want to make the world a better place for our children, but not anyone else's. We want to be able to earn a living, support our children, but then we want to change all the rules when it's time to retire. Build a school! Build a hospital! Build a halfway house for wayward teens! Hey wait a minute, though. Don't build it in my backyard.

After the "old people watching the sunset comment," my hand shot up. I waved it in the air like a second grader, ooh-ooh-oohing to give the answer. But I had to wait my turn to be recognized by the board, a whole panel of zoning professors. When the man finally stopped talking, the board allowed me to speak.

"Contrary to what's been said, I have to differ with this definition of Squaw Lake. First of all, Sandy Point Resort has been in existence and providing means for families well before anyone in this room was old and retired. And why any of you want to deny us the opportunity to earn our living and raise our family in an honest and legitimate manner is hard for me to understand. All we want to do with this house is legally rent it out on a week-to-week basis, and continue to support the economy of the Northwoods. Last time I checked, tourism was a legitimate and important part of this community. I'm asking you to not believe the garbage floating around about high-rises and RV parks. Please listen to me. You're looking at the so-called Sandy Point Developers and I'm telling you our plans."

The board did not seem impressed. While I silently broke into applause for myself, the room remained quiet and the faces of the board members looked toward their watches. We had run out of time. They were not ready to vote, and scheduled a second hearing.

In the week that followed, another lake neighbor got involved. Even though he didn't support the rezoning, he suggested a compromise. He drew up a series of restrictions to act as an amendment—a sort of put-your-money-where-your-mouth-is clause—to our rezoning application. It outlined our intent to remodel the house and not turn it into anything the neighbors feared. It further suggested that we keep the two properties separate and if we ever sold the Lakeview property we would again have it rezoned back to a single-family residential status. We agreed to this clause, hired an attorney to draw up the wording and were ready to present the paragraph to the community and the board.

At the second hearing it was a brand new day. The weather had improved to look and feel more like spring, and people no longer suffered from cabin fever. When the sun made a lasting appearance and the snow melted, there were other things to think about. Our new clause was presented, and for the first time the board seemed impressed. Then the president of the Squaw Lake Association stood and said he supported the rezoning of Lakeview Lodge. No one in the room seemed to have any other objections until a rather plump young man in a gray suit, red tie, and the word "lawyer" stamped on his forehead, stood to address the board.

"We still have strenuous objections to the rezoning of the . . ." he said. Obviously, some of our neighbors, including the locals whose relatives had written us the threatening letter two summers earlier, didn't want to give up the fight. (Maybe they felt they owed it to "their people" to make trouble for us.) But on that spring day, no one on the zoning board had time for more trouble.

The crowd sighed and the board chairman dismissed the lawyer with a wave. The vote went in our favor. When the meeting ended, several people approached us with wishes of good luck and congratulations. One man, who attended the meeting only to witness the process, came and asked for advice. He had an upcoming zoning hearing regarding a storage facility business that was under construction. The neighbor to his south had given him a "not in my backyard" argument, and his spirits were lifted by the result of our hearing.

Ah, neighbors. City or country, you can't choose 'em. You can't kill 'em.

As the years have passed and our neighbors saw that we didn't put up the high-rises they feared or allow airplanes to land next to them, they also found we haven't yet gone belly up. On the day we paved Sandy Point Lane, the road leading into our resort, one man met Mike at the end of the road and scratched his chin. "You must be doing better than I thought," he said.

It must be said that *all* our neighbors have been civil to us whenever we've encountered them at the road or mailbox. Our dogs, in particular, loved one group who patrolled the road each morning by picking up trash. The dogs often accompanied them on morning walks and happily ate the biscuits they carried in their pockets. Whenever Luna or Dakotah escaped from the kennel or got bored hanging out in front of our home, we were sure to find her over on the front porch of our neighbor's place. (I've always believed that when children and animals like you, you've got to be okay.) And sometimes on a still day when I sit alone on a bench at the end of our main dock, I hear the beautiful sounds of a neighborhood piano traveling freely over the water and filling the air with music. There's an extremely talented musician somewhere on the lake, and as I enjoy the dreamy soundtrack behind my perfect view I quietly thank her.

We have several other neighbors from the south end of the lake who drop by regularly to visit or play disc golf, and a few of them use our cabins for guest-overflow at their lake homes or rent boats and motors from us. Just like the neighbors of folklore they drop by to check on us after a storm goes through, or to ask for advice on things like septic systems and electrical problems. We've met a great number of wonderful people, and we're always happy when they stop by since we rarely have the opportunity to leave the Resort during the busy summer season. We don't even go to the annual Lake Association meeting because it's always held on a Saturday in July, and we just can't get away on turnover day.

We are particularly sorry we missed the meeting during the summer of 2001, when our fellow Squaw Lake neighbors shared a common concern about a political movement that was suddenly gathering steam. It had to do with the name of our lake. In line with our country's current obsession with political correctness, to the surprise of many the word "squaw," to some, is an offensive word. Every time I read an article on the subject, I learn a different origin of the word squaw. It's either Iroquois or Algonquin and its consistent definition is: "Indian woman" or "wife." Almost everyone I've asked over the years—including women of Native American heritage—believes this is the intended meaning of the word. But someone, somehow, made it a nasty word. Its derogatory connotation is consistently attributed to the French, who apparently corrupted the word to mean "female genitalia."

Now personally, I don't have the slightest problem with female genitalia. I can and will utter the word "vagina" without blushing, and freely admit that I have one. Having given birth to two daughters, I'm willing to bet that it was the first thing that anyone either saw or noticed about me, as I distinctly recall the female genitalia that greeted my curious eyes especially during the birth of our second daughter, Camille. I had the opportunity to pull her from my body as the doctor guided my hands under her tiny shoulders after they emerged from the darkness of my womb. He asked if I was willing to "pull out the baby," and I was more than happy to do so. And what was the first thing about this child that came into focus? You guessed it. Female genitalia. And in my opinion, it was a beautiful sight.

Of course I realize that there are many, many slang words used to try to pollute and demean women of all races and creeds. I've cringed at the sound of various derogatory words commonly used for the word vagina, but have also used them to prove a point from time to time. After all, aren't they ultimately just words? I'm amazed that as a society we continually give words such incredible power. We now have terms like "the n-word," and yet we see movie after movie with African-American cast members uttering the taboo word, using it almost as an endearment. It's okay for some, but not others. (Isn't that a form of discrimination?) We have a lesbian community, once offended by the term "dyke," who has embraced the word by taking out the sting and making it its own. I say, "good for them." There are many examples. The word "bitch" comes to mind. It's defined as a female dog and is supposed to be offensive to women as well. But I know many women (myself included) who in some circumstances wear this name like a badge of honor.

Hey, maybe that might be a good new name for our lake: Bitch Lake. It's got a certain, *je ne ce'st qua*, don't you think?

This entire flap about female genitalia—Native-American female genitalia to be specific—is just nuts. I'm willing to bet all female genitalia looks pretty much the same no matter what outside skin color you have. Women, in general, could probably be called a lot worse. And without a doubt, our lake could probably have a more offensive name. I don't understand why we need to succumb to a mere connotation of an otherwise perfectly acceptable word.

I've seen the *Vagina Monologues*, a popular stage presentation written by Eve Ensler that celebrates female genitalia and cites possibly every word used to euphemize it. (For the record, during the version I saw in London, "squaw" was not on the list). This show, which has not only won awards and the attention of numerous celebrities who flock to the stage to recite the provocative, funny and poignant monologues, has also strived to make the term "vagina" something we can say out loud without embarrassment. Why on earth should the door in which we've all gone through in order to face life on this planet offend us?

Nevertheless, I don't want to be insensitive to anyone who is truly offended by the word "squaw." And in spite of the fact that our Lake Association was something like ninety percent against the renaming of our lake, creek, and surrounding roads, the last I heard a committee in the Wisconsin Legislature was on a squaw-squashing pioneer trail making its way east from California through the Bad Lands and Minnesota and into our state. The United States has some 1,050 places using the name Squaw and in Wisconsin it names lakes, bays, creeks, islands, mounds, points and waterfowl areas in twenty counties.

When the Squaw Lake Association asked its members to come up with a list of potential new names for our lake, I took the job seriously. A lot of people suggested we find a word that sounded like "squaw," or at least come up with another name that began with the letter "s", in order to "S"implify the process. I thought that was too easy. Naming something is a huge responsibility and an incredible and unique opportunity. During my travels over the years and particularly when I've come across a clever name printed on a map or a road sign, I've often felt a sort of ridiculous disappointment for being born too late to have had the chance to pick out names for things like mountains, gulches and lakes. My disappointment was eased when I gave birth and, along with my husband, we took great pleasure in choosing names for our children.

I'm constantly asked about how we came up with the name "Willow" for our first-born. I've lost count of the number of people who have referred to the Ron Howard film, *Willow*, a movie I finally saw for the first time last year after paying far too much money on E-Bay for a used copy in pretty poor shape. Apparently, it's an out-of-print cult flick or some such thing. So the movie was not the inspiration. I begin the saga of our daughter's name by reflecting on a short story I started writing years ago about a little girl who lived in the forest. I named her Willow after a tree, because she was long-limbed and graceful. I never finished the story, and can't even remember what it was about. But I realized while writing it that I lived in the wrong setting—a busy city, in the shadow of an oil refinery, no less—to stimulate my creativity. So the story was tabled and never completed. Then one day while I was very pregnant I made my daily walk down Sandy Point Lane (this was after Mike had banned my use of cross-country skis because I had fallen and couldn't get up), and it dawned on me that I finally lived in the perfect setting for the rebirth of my Willow. And *our* Willow arrived in March, which was still the dead of winter in the Northwoods. March, however, is a month I have always associated with spring. And I learned that in the spring the willow tree is always the first to bud. The name was perfect.

For a journalist, every article begins with research. When I sat down to work on a new name for our lake I learned by reading several books on local culture purchased from touristy book stores in town, that the Ojibway culture has a rich history of soul searching rituals used to understand the origin of nature; of life, existence and death. By using insight, dreams or vision quests, through ceremonies, they reenacted revelations to pay respect to all humans, plants, animals and the earth. One of the most important rituals is the naming ceremony or *Wauweendaussowin*. Names for children, for example, were often not chosen until several years after birth, as urgency was less important than choosing a name deemed appropriate for the being.

With my newfound respect for this beautiful culture's naming process and my awareness of the derogatory meaning of the word squaw, which had become impossible to disregard, I soon believed that the name of the lake should indeed be changed. But I didn't want to completely disregard the history of the lake known as Squaw, which carried that name for as long as anyone could remember.

I insisted on looking at the word "squaw" in a positive light, and re-

ferred to its most common meaning, "Indian woman." I thought to coun-
teract the negative meaning of this word, the lake's new name should rep-
resent an honorable term for a Native American woman. For example, the
Ojibway word for woman is *Akw é*. So how about Lake Awk é? Or perhaps
more simply, Maiden Lake? Other ideas I presented to the Lake Association were Grandmother Lake, Medicine Woman Lake and Elder Lake.

One neighbor wrote to say he liked the sound of Elder Lake, but that
Medicine Woman Lake and East Medicine Woman Lake Road might be a
little too much to write out in the return address corner of his envelopes.
He had a good point.

As far as we know, no one else liked any of my suggestions. We're not
even aware of any leading contenders or whether or not the property owners on the lake will have a vote on the issue. Apparently, when it comes to
naming things most of us will just have to fulfill that need by naming our
children and our pets.

After the summer, the issue seemed to fade. My understanding is that
there's still a committee in Madison planning to make a decision and we'll
be informed when it's time to reprint our checks, return address labels and
marketing literature. Meanwhile, I am completely out of resort brochures
and I'll be darned if I'm going to invest in the cost of printing 5,000 new
four-color brochures with the wrong lake name.

In spite of whether or not we have common interests or even common goals for our environment, with our neighbors it seems we must always be on our guard. While the man who drew up the petition against us
during our rezoning effort has left his Northwoods home with a for sale
sign in the yard, the man who suggested we draw up the restriction amendment to our zoning application has not stopped his campaign to have every
property on the lake rezoned to single-family residential status. And a few
years after we bought Lakeview Lodge, we tore down three of the old out-
buildings that acted as storage sheds and garages and replaced them with
one, big garage. Someone, we don't know who, complained to the zoning

administrator that we violated the covenant of our deed and had built another rental unit. This was simply not true.

I read in the local newspaper the other day that in the town of Minocqua where a clothing store was under construction, the business owner of the abandoned building next to it filed a complaint that the new building was closer to the road than his building. Construction was halted, a lot of paperwork generated, only to discover there weren't any setback restrictions in that zone and, therefore, no laws were broken. So, work continued. I could illustrate a hundred other examples of neighbors giving each other a hard time over the most trivial things. Suffice it to say, some neighbors just don't have anything better to do than to play the role of Gladys Kravitz. They live everywhere, not just in the Northwoods of Wisconsin, and not just next to resorts. They're out there and ready to make your business their own. We've learned to have a good lawyer on hand, one who is ready to fight for us, and even issue a restraining order if necessary.

You just never know when someone is going to get bored with his or her own life and try to put a damper on your "dream life."

People Can Be Jerks

One of the mottos I developed as a resort owner is the very pessimistic notion that "not only can people be jerks, but they *are* jerks." I decided to go into each busy summer season believing this strictly as a matter of self-defense. If I expected every person who approached me to say something jerky, I figured I'd spend most of my time being surprised and delighted when they were kind and friendly. I prefer that feeling over the shock and horror I've experienced in the past due to some of the things they've said to me.

For example, I was shocked on the morning a woman barged into my kitchen and asked for information about a cottage that was for sale on the lake. It was early, and I was pouring a cup of coffee while my nursing-bra had not yet been refastened following my baby's first morning meal.

"Hey there," she said, "what can you tell me about that property down the road?"

"Excuse me?" I asked, nearly dropping the coffee pot. "Who are you, and what are you doing in my kitchen?"

"Isn't this the lodge?" she asked. "This is a resort, isn't it?"

"This is my home," I said. "Didn't you see the sign saying 'PRIVATE' on the door you opened?"

"No, I didn't," she replied, without an apology. "But do you know how much they're asking for that place? It's just down the road." She stretched her arm and pointed toward the living room, which was filled with un-folded laundry and other neglected clutter (all of which would have been put away had I been expecting to give the weekly house tour).

Not only did I know nothing about the cottage for sale, I couldn't get beyond the notion that there was a complete stranger standing in my kitchen where I stood with my boob hanging out of my pajamas. Like a politician unwilling to expose certain aspects of her personal life, this was just unacceptable to me. I used her same outstretched arm motion, pointed to the front door and told her to leave.

"Well, I was just looking for some information," she said with a whine. "You don't have to be rude!"

A part of me knew people could be jerks from the time I was very young—an adolescent, to be more precise. With legs as long and skinny as mine, it was an invitation to the jerks to exercise their freedom of unkind speech. I was called more nicknames than I can remember. Legs, Stick, Daddy Long Legs, Leggy, Twiggy, Tweety Bird—and these were just because of the legs. Board (carpenter's dream), Flatsy and Titless were sometimes thrown in as well because those two stick legs of mine were like straight arrows pointing right up to my lack of a chest.

I may have been skinny, but I made up for it by being tough. I was blessed with a lot of natural athletic ability and had an older brother who let me play with him and the guys in the tree-lined streets of our suburban neighborhood. I learned to talk my way into any game and better yet, talk my kind brother, the self-appointed quarterback, into actually passing the ball to me. I had something to prove to those boys and they accepted me as a regular player.

In sixth grade I made the seventh grade girl's volleyball team, and by eighth grade I was the team captain. The only other thing elementary school offered was cheerleading for the boy's basketball team, so I tried out for that and made it, too. Then, inspired by Billie Jean King beating Bobby Riggs on the tennis court, a group of girls tried out for the boy's track team, and we made it. A year later, Title IX was enacted, a bill requiring gender equality in sports, and we no longer had to prove ourselves worthy to compete with or against the boys. But I already thought I was as good as any boy at just about anything I wanted to do. It helped, too, that I grew to a lean and respectable five-foot, ten-inches and managed honor roll grades in school.

I learned that the best defense against anyone—any jerk, male or female—is to make no extra room for intimidation. When I was in college someone told me if I was ever in an interview situation being questioned by a potential employer or intimidator, I should try to visualize that person on the toilet, sick with diarrhea. And while I couldn't bring myself to draw that picture (it's bad enough when *I'm* sick with diarrhea), it was a springboard for the simple notion that everyone you deal with is just human.

Unfortunately, humans can sometimes be jerks. It must be said that the majority of our guests, over ninety percent, are perfectly lovely people. Many return year after year and we are truly delighted to see them. I, in fact, enjoy cleaning the cabins when I know who is expected to arrive for the week. I think about them and wonder how big the kids will be or how the weather will be for their vacation. I anticipate their arrivals with an excitement on a par with the way I feel when a family member is due to show up.

The good news about the jerks is they aren't the types who come back year after year. They like to cause trouble or issue complaints and leave, only to blame you for everything and go cause more problems for someone else on their next vacation.

Again, most of the people who come to the resort are nice and very easy to talk to. But occasionally there have been people who were so intimidating they made my knees knock when I developed the courage to look them in the face. My father-in-law was that kind of man. I had tremendous respect for him, but he scared me. While his devil's advocate approach to any conversation was both challenging and frustrating, it was because of him that Mike and I put together a thoughtful and ultimately successful business plan for Sandy Point Resort.

"This business is losing money," he roared after looking at the financial statements of the previous owners. "What are you going to do to turn it around?"

Aside from always telling us, "You've got to get bigger," Mike's dad, a successful businessman himself, had a number of practical and important suggestions. For example, he insisted we take the issue of liability and insurance very seriously. He said if you can't afford to have an expensive and wide reaching umbrella liability policy on your resort, you couldn't be in business. Because along with the philosophy that people are jerks, an important sidebar is that people who are jerks *will* sue you if they get the chance.

I'm told that in medical school students learn in the chapter on malpractice insurance to approach the subject of lawsuits not as an "if" but as a "when." A book I used as a guide to develop a business plan for the resort made the same statement. "The question isn't whether you'll be sued, it's when." It said that owners of small businesses are among the most vulnerable, and in the case of an accident on our property the jury wouldn't look at us as simply Mike and Michele Cozzens, but as the owners of Sandy Point Resort—which is a marketable asset.

We live in an age where malpractice attorneys advertise on television at all hours of the day. Even the back cover of our small Northwoods phone book has a four-color ad. "Have you been injured? Wronged? Don't like the way someone treated you? . . . " The message is, "It's NOT your fault. Make someone else pay your bills." There are so many lawyers in this country that almost every citizen is bound to have a distant or even close family relative hanging an attorney's shingle to dangle in the winds of litigation.

Our first experience with a lawsuit happened early in our tenure as resort owners. And because the personal injury lawyers for the plaintiff asked for every dime of both our homeowner's and commercial liability policies, we're relieved we invested in appropriate insurance coverage. If we hadn't had those policies, we believe they would have put a price tag on our resort and sued for that amount.

It started on a warm August afternoon, a day where you could practically hear the old Hamm's Beer jingle beating a drum in the background,

I'm Living Your Dream Life

"From the land of sky blue waters . . . " The sky was azure-blue and the waters of Squaw Lake reflected the surrounding trees like a mirror. The beach was full of swimmers and the lake was full of boaters. It was the summer of 1995, when our first child, Willow, was five months old. Determined to lose those extra pounds from carrying her for nine months, I took every opportunity that summer to swim and water-ski when the weather permitted. And the weather permitted that day.

We had friends and family staying in two of the cabins. Mike's brother, Jeff, and his family were there, and an old high school friend of Mike's named Charlie and his family were there as well. We always like having friends and family at the resort because it gives us an excuse not to work. With friends around we use the lake and disc golf course a little more than usual. That day we all took turns water-skiing behind our boat, and Charlie and I even had fun skiing double.

At the time the resort had eight units, and typical of the prime summer weeks, they were all occupied. Two families, who made the bookings together, rented two of the smaller cabins, numbers three and four. They were friends from college, I believe, and one family lived in central Wisconsin, the other in Minnesota. Meeting at Sandy Point required about a four-hour drive for each family, and they thought it would be a good location for a reunion.

I liked these people when they checked in on the previous Saturday. They were young—our age—well-educated and good-looking. As we do with all our guests before we get to know them, we named them according to their cabin numbers. These people were Mr. and Mrs. Cabin Three, and Mr. and Mrs. Cabin Four. They each had young children and were clearly happy about being on vacation together.

But disaster struck. On Thursday, they rented one of our boats. It was a tri-hull by Glastron with an outboard motor, a boat we called the Avocado because of its memorably fashionable 1970s color. Once our personal ski boat, we decided to rent it after we found a good used ski boat a few months earlier. Although we had rented the Avocado three or four times prior to that day, most of our equipment rental experience had been with eight-horsepower outboard motors, which guests use with the rowboats we provide each cabin. We used a rental agreement form that explains safe operating procedures and contains a liability waiver.

The men approached me while I was at the beach. "Can we rent your ski boat this afternoon?" asked Mr. Cabin Four. "We just want to have the true Northwoods lake experience and today is a beautiful day."

"Sure," I said. "Come up to the office and we'll fill out the paperwork." I needed to bring Willow inside anyway, to change her into a diaper and out of her wet, sandy clothes.

They followed Willow and me up the hill and waited at the front desk while I set Willow down on a towel in the middle of the living room. I gave them the form.

"Do you have an inner tube or something we can use, too?" they asked. "We'd really like to pull the kids, and they're too young for skiing."

I said they could use our tube and towrope, listed the items on the form, but didn't charge them. (I liked them. It was a favor.) They were in a hurry to get back down to the lake, but I told them they had to go through a safety check and operation instructions with Mike, which was our standard procedure for outboard motors.

"Why? Is it going to explode?" joked Mr. Cabin Four.

The explosion had happened two days earlier. The men and the kids were out playing on the disc golf course just before dinnertime, while their wives stayed behind in cabin three to prepare the evening meal. Apparently, neither woman had experienced operating a propane-fueled oven before, and in spite of the instructions we gave them about how to light it, one turned on the gas and then closed the oven door for some time prior to lighting the match. What ensued was a bang that from my house sounded like a sonic boom. It blew with so much force that all the framed pictures and decorations fell off the cabin walls. Even though the noise was very loud and certainly frightening, no one was hurt.

Mr. Cabin Three didn't want us to know but his wife told us the next day that he was so upset when he heard his family had caused an explosion, he had a panic attack and was taken to the hospital. My recollection is that he had some sort of heart condition, requiring medication from time to time.

But he was fine. Everyone was fine and we all laughed it off. That day we made a mental note to remind and re-remind all guests staying in those cabins how to light the ovens. I didn't yet know that people are jerks, but was learning that they can definitely be dumb.

Then in the middle of our joking and kidding my phone rang and I left the office to answer it. When I came back a few minutes later, they were gone and they had left the form on the counter. I saw it sitting there and went back inside to tend to Willow. They didn't sign it.

Hours passed and I went back and forth between the house and the beach, keeping my eye on the resort and my baby. Mike was working the lakefront, spending most of his time socializing and monitoring the lake activities.

Then suddenly from the house I heard a man yell, "Call a doctor! We need a doctor!" The voice was urgent and serious and it came from the beach. Instinctively, I grabbed the phone and ran outside where I came face-to-face with Mrs. Cabin Three.

"Call 9-1-1," she said. "It's really bad."

We didn't have 9-1-1 service, so I raced back into the house to get the emergency number for an ambulance. Nervously, I called the number without even knowing what happened.

"There's been some kind of boating accident," I said. "We need an ambulance." Then I explained who I was and where we were located. "Hurry!" I said. "It's very serious."

It was Mrs. Cabin Four who was injured and it *was* bad. By the time I got to the lakefront, she was stretched out on the edge of our dock with my brother-in-law, Jeff, the neurosurgeon, and Charlie's wife, Jean, a nurse, tending to her. Her eyes were wide and frightened, her face as pale as the white dock on which she laid.

Except for the group at the end of the dock, the beach, which had earlier been filled with activity, was eerily quiet. Jeff's wife had gathered the thirty or so children who were on the property at the time, and took them to the Recreation House to watch a video. She too was a nurse, and knew the injury Mrs. Cabin Four had suffered was not something children were meant to see. Everything on the lake had come to a stop. Everything except for the Avocado, which was about half a mile off shore. Abandoned, it cruised in slow circles. Around and around it went, like a kite without a tail, an unpiloted boat with the inner tube trailing closely behind.

The story they reported was that Mr. Cabin Three was driving and Mrs. Cabin Four was the passenger. Her husband rode the inner tube. They went around in circles in the bay area near the resort and like a lot of tubers, played "crack the whip," turning in tight circles so that Mr. Cabin Four was thrown across the wake for a more thrilling ride.

"But then I hit a wave or something," said Mr. Cabin Three, "and I let go of the wheel."

Just as you don't let propane build up pressure inside an oven before you light a match, you should never, never let go of the wheel of a moving boat. Predictably, the boat yawed hard, went up on its side and dumped both the driver and his passenger, Mrs. Cabin Four, into the lake. She wore a life preserver, but was slow to surface and establish her bearings. When the boat circled back, her arm got caught in the prop.

Neighbors who were on the lake in their boat witnessed the accident and immediately raced to the scene. They rescued the three victims and knew that Mrs. Cabin Four was in big trouble. Blood from her badly torn arm covered the floor of their boat as they brought her to the dock at Sandy Point.

It was pure luck that a neurosurgeon was within shouting distance. As people shouted his name, "Jeff! Jeff!" Charlie's wife, Jean, who had a son named Jeff on the property thought the panic was surrounding her child. She ran from her cabin and found herself assisting Jeff the doctor, while he tried to stabilize Mrs. Cabin Four.

Meanwhile, the clock ticked and the ambulance seemed to take forever. They say it always seems like a lot longer when you're waiting during an emergency situation, but I had my eye on the clock. I called again with more specific directions and the dispatcher assured me they were on their way. I drove to the end of our lane and parked, waiting for the sound of the siren. Finally, I heard it and I directed them to the scene.

Perhaps it was my heightened sense of urgency, but this seemed to be a lazy crew. They showed no sense of exigency or concern. They were reluctant to drive their vehicle down the road to the lake and it was I who carried the wooden stretcher to the shore. "Come on!" I screamed at them. "She may have lost her arm!"

When Jeff learned that the ambulance crew didn't even have an I-V, which she desperately needed, he rode with them to the hospital to insure she was in good hands. Without his help it's possible she may have died on our dock.

But she didn't die. She was flown to another hospital and underwent a series of grafts and surgeries and recovered some, but not all use of her hand and arm. For a woman with three young children, one of whom still needed help getting dressed and fed, this was a terrible situation.

"You're going to get sued," said Jeff when he returned from the hospital.

"You think so?" we asked.

"Count on it."

Earlier, while Mr. Cabin Four and his children were still on property he jokingly told us we'd being hearing from his lawyer. When he saw my face drop, he reached out and put his hands on my shoulders. "I would never do that," he said. "We're not like that."

It was probably his lawyer who told him to "never say never." We were served the following Father's Day, right about the time Jeff and Jean received thank you notes in their mailboxes. Their friend, Mr. Cabin Three and the driver of the boat, was also served. He, in fact, was named first in the lawsuit, and we, as owners of the boat, were named second. I'm pretty sure the boat and motor manufacturers were named as well.

I can honestly say that all along our real concern was for the health and healing of Mrs. Cabin Four. Her scared, suffering eyes looked right through me that day on the dock, and my heart nearly beat out of my chest in fear for her. I realized they were having a wonderful afternoon with their friends and family, the same way we were. And suddenly, everything—including her entire future—had changed.

Since we had insurance, technically (while we were named in the suit) it was our insurance company who had to foot the bill. The company representative instructed us to do everything the hired lawyer told us to do.

Mr. Cabin Four, who like a well-brought-up guilt-ridden Catholic, called us during the ordeal to assure us they had no ill feelings towards us. "We don't have anything against you personally," he said one day. "It's just that we don't like the attitude of your insurance company. We're not suing you, we're suing *them*!"

That old line.

His phone call had the opposite affect on me than what I believed was his intent. He tried to make me feel better, but I felt a lot worse. If he didn't hold anything against us and felt it wasn't our fault, then why did we have to answer to charges of negligence where the boat was concerned? According to his attorney, he had accused us of not properly maintaining the Avocado and knowingly renting faulty equipment. He insisted we offered little, if any, safety instructions and that the boat was clearly in ill-repair. We were subjected to months and months of taped depositions and had to make the boat and our property available to investigator after investigator—from our insurance company, from their lawyer, from the boat and motor companies, from his friend—the driver's insurance company. They called our clients and friends; they knocked on our neighbor's doors. They tried to find out whether or not we were negligent scumbags and we didn't like it one bit.

The fact that we were under investigation made us nervous. What else might happen at the resort to cause another insurance claim? For example, lightning struck our well pump after the boating accident and it needed to be replaced at a cost of several thousand dollars. Normally this is something covered by our insurance—but not any more. Once this suit finally settled (for over a million dollars) our insurance agent warned us that any additional claims might lead to the company dropping us as clients.

So while Mr. Cabin Four wanted to believe that the suit really didn't have anything to do with us, it was a major inconvenience and continues to be a threat to out ability to stay in business. Yes, we weren't physically hurt and have full use of all of our limbs, but we are the operators of a small business and that, in the eyes of our litigious society, is a marketable asset. We've got to protect it like we protect our children.

It must be said that the families we called the Cabin Three and Cabin Four families were *not* jerks. It was a jerky move—literally—that led Mr. Cabin Three to let go of the steering wheel of the boat and cause the accident that nearly killed his friend, but what we learned from this experience is that "If it CAN happen, it *will.*" And to always be prepared.

As for this next story, the guy was just a jerk, plain and simple.

The birch trees in northern Wisconsin are disappearing. It's a sad but true statement that before too long, the birch tree may be a rare sight in the Northwoods. When we bought Sandy Point Resort we were told that both a blight and a birch bore were eating and destroying them, and that they'd "all be gone within ten years." Well, there are still hundreds of healthy birch trees on our property alone, so it doesn't look as dire as all that. But since living on the property, we have watched the disintegration of several birch trees. Once a branch of the tree is infected, leaves no longer bloom—and that's the first sign of a dying tree. Then the texture of the bark softens and separates, and when branches fall to the ground the pieces explode like shredded wheat. Sometimes on windy days I hear a crackle in the distance that sounds like popping popcorn, and know it's another ill-fated birch tree about to drop one more section.

Healthy birch bark can be very useful. The Chippewa Indians, who are native to our area, have made practical and decorative items out of birch bark for years. Native American lore indicates the tree is blessed for the good of the human race. And this is why "lightning never strikes the birch tree, and why anything wrapped in the bark will not decay." Birch bark is used for making canoes, house coverings, containers, utensils, and in many other ways. Tourists love to collect pieces and bring them home as souvenirs. Kids, who can also be jerks, love to peel the bark. If I catch them doing it, the Mother Superior habit comes on at once.

"Do you realize you're peeling the skin off a live thing?" I say. "How would you like it if I came up to you and peeled your skin?"

I then tell them that the Indians, who found that only live trees with "summer bark" were useful, never sacrificed a birch without honoring it. Typically, an offering of tobacco was sprinkled in place of the felled tree. The kids don't have tobacco, but I suggest they take the worms, rocks, snails or candy out of their pockets and set them at the base of a tree they just damaged.

Kids aren't the only ones who damage the trees. Each summer we have several small and at least one big storm. These characteristically Midwestern storms come from the west with drum-roll-like fanfare. The sky grows dark with a greenish black hue, and the wind kicks up whitecaps on the hematite-colored lake. Thunder growls in the distance and the sky lights up as if someone is waving a flashlight, signaling in Morse code. As the storm makes its way to us, the lightning streaks across the sky in jagged bolts and thunder roars so powerfully that the windows rattle. Tree branches always fall and help keep our kindling supply healthy for the never-ending camp-fires made by our guests. Because of their deterioration, the birch are hit particularly hard. The Native Americans may believe that this tree was never struck by lightning, but the wind does as much if not more damage. Some wind storms are so strong that birch trees with five, two-foot-wide trunks sharing the same root system have been completely uprooted, leaving a six-foot by six-foot hole in the sandy soil.

By the way, these storms also include a lot of rain. It comes down in sheets, which makes it seem like you're looking through plastic when look-ing out the window. It erodes the sandy soil and the root systems of the trees, wipes out the beach, sinks the boats, and makes for a constant main-tenance chore with our railroad tie step paths.

One summer when we had an average summer storm, there was a man staying on property who was the guest of a guest. In other words I didn't know his name, other than to call him the guest of Mr. Cabin Five. In spite of our policy that all persons and cars must be signed in since our facilities are for registered guests only, many people feel, of course, that the "rules" do not apply to them. But this man and Mr. Cabin Five clearly were among those who were absent on the day in kindergarten when their teacher pre-sented the lesson about the importance of following the rules.

In addition to security issues that make it important for us to know who is on the property at all times, our cabin rates are based on certain occupancy levels. We have limits as to the numbers of people allowed in each cabin, and charge extra beyond the cabin's basic occupancy rate. Wear and tear on the facilities—especially the septic systems—is a real issue for us.

At registration we ask guests to inform us of any visitors they plan to have during the week. We mention the extra charges and ask them if they'd like to pay in advance or have their guests pay upon arrival. I've learned to always ask about how and when the fees will be paid after one guest be-came angry with me for informing his in-laws that there was an extra charge for their visit. "We didn't want them to know!" he said. "And now you've made them feel bad."

I didn't recognize the guest of Mr. Cabin Five when he rang my doorbell the day after the storm. It was early afternoon. He was an older man, a guy who looked like he might have once served in the military during one of the wars, and was now retired and played a lot of golf. In other words, gray hair poked out from underneath a white cap, and he wore a golf uniform—a collared shirt and print slacks. I guessed he was someone off the street who had stopped to either tour the resort or ask for a brochure, or saw the sign for the disc golf course and thought it read "discount golf."

"May I help you?" I asked.

"Yeah," he said. "I'd like to know the name of your insurance carrier."

"My insurance carrier?"

"Yes, because of the storm yesterday, there was some damage to my car."

"Wait a minute," I said. "I'm sorry you've had some difficulty, but are you telling me the damage to your car happened here? Are you staying here?"

"I'm not sure if it happened here because I just noticed it this morning when we were out driving around. But I parked over there by Cabin Five last night, and it must have happened here. There's birch scrap all around where I was parked."

As the hair on the back of my neck tingled, and the temperature near my temples elevated, I stepped outside. I thought of several questions. What time did you park there? Was it before, during or after the storm? And perhaps the question burning the most adrenaline in my stomach was: who the *hell* are you anyway?

Instead I asked, "Is the vehicle you're talking about registered here?"

"No, it isn't," he said. "But I'm staying here with my friend and I'm quite sure he is registered."

"So, you're telling me that some damage happened to your vehicle, an unregistered vehicle on our property, and you're not sure whether or not it happened here but you want the name of my insurance carrier so you can file a claim against us?"

"It's going to cost a few hundred bucks to get that dent out of my roof," he said adamantly.

"Well then, sir," I said, "I suggest you contact your own insurance carrier to help take care of the repair bill. I'm assuming, of course, that you have car insurance?"

"Of course I do!" he snapped. "But I've got a $500 deductible. And I shouldn't have to pay for that. You should. It was your tree!"

"Sir," I said, by this time quite annoyed, "I'll come down and have a look at your car, but I truly don't believe my insurance company is going to take responsibility for an accident that you say may or may not have happened on this property. You said you didn't even know if it was our tree."

"Well that's just not right," he yelled. "I want the name of your agent and I want it right now."

"I'm not giving it to you," I said turning around. We were still in the middle of the boating accident case, and there was no way I was going to involve our insurance company in another matter that was absolutely trivial in comparison. If he wanted to sue us, just let him try! At that point, I was the girl with the flat chest and skinny legs who had already taken far too much abuse.

"Well then you should provide covered parking for your guests with all these damn trees around here!" he shouted after me.

"Thanks for the suggestion," I said without turning around. I wished I was a VCR and he was a tape, so I could push the eject button and spit him out. How could I toss this guy off the grounds? What were my rights in this scenario?

I had virtually no sympathy for him. I could care less about his car or his situation because of his dictatorial attitude and his stupidity in presenting the case the way he did. "I don't know if it happened here or not . . . "

As far as I was concerned, he was trespassing on our property and had no rights other than to get back in his dented car—a minor dent at that—and leave.

Sure enough, about two months later we received a call from his insurance carrier who called to investigate. We told him we took no responsibility for the damage since his client said he wasn't sure where the accident happened. He asked for the name of our agent and we didn't give it to him.

We never heard from them again.

Big incidents, small incidents. The jerks get all the airtime, and there's something wrong with this. But I get off on a little gossip now and then, and I talk about the jerks because they keep me on my toes and prepared for the next incident. I think of them as educational tools. And let's face it, when you open up your home and property to anyone who wants to pay you to use it, you're going to put up with a few people you wouldn't want to invite again to your dining room table. As I've always said to Mike, you don't have to like everyone and, more importantly, everyone doesn't have to like you.

One time there was a lady who had her nose turned up from the second she stepped out of her car. In spite of my effort to make eye contact and greet her with a smile, she was clearly one of those ladies who was dragged by the hair and resentful that she wasn't on a cruise ship somewhere instead of in the woods with her family. To me, her expression said, "I'm trouble. Just watch how many things I'll find wrong with your resort."

Well, as with a lot of my first impressions, I was wrong. She turned out to be fairly nice. But there was one incident I remember very clearly, because it led me to make up signs for all the cabins regarding the bed linens. It was Sunday, the guests' first full day and the day I like to spend time at the beach with my kids when the weather is nice. When I got to the shore, I noticed two bed quilts from her cabin spread out in the sand. Wet kids ran over them, and coolers sat on top of them as if they were picnic blankets.

"I'm sorry ma'am," I said to her, "but I noticed you're using the bed quilts as picnic blankets . . . "

And before I could finish, she snapped back at me, "I'll WASH them!"
She didn't.

Another guest once came to my front door midweek. Frankly, this skinny,
pasty-white guy was a nerd. He was the dad of the family, but clearly did
not come up to the woods to spend time fishing with his sons. I don't think
he left the cabin other than to come to my door with a complaint.

"The water's not hot enough," he whined.

"The water in the cabin?" I asked.

"Yeah. I can't get the dishes clean and sterilized in lukewarm water, and
I don't want my kids to get germs."

"I'm sorry," I said. "I think someone complained that the water was
too hot and they scalded themselves in the shower. So Mike turned down
the thermostat a couple weeks ago."

"Well, I wouldn't know about the shower," he said. "I haven't used it
yet."

Yuck. Here was a man concerned about his kids drinking from cups
washed in lukewarm water, but he hadn't bathed in four days. I sent Mike to
his cabin with instructions to make the water nice and hot.

People have complained about wrinkled sheets, not enough bed pillows, the smell of propane and pine, the lack of water pressure, bad TV
reception, and toilet paper that wasn't soft enough for their tender bottoms. They're disappointed by the complete lack of cellular phone reception, and that the electronic clocks on their appliances are blinking due to
the frequent power surges. Completely ignoring the "no smoking" signs in
the cabins and our request that they use the screen porches or smoke outside, they light up anyway and blow smoke until the curtains and upholstery
reek. Once, a guest who obviously liked to smoke in bed, used the top
drawer of the wall-mounted nightstand as an ashtray and failed to empty it
before leaving. People cut their toenails in places other than the bathrooms,
and leave the scraps for us to clean out of the carpet. They complain about

the mosquitoes, and often blame us for the rain. They blame us when their kids fall down and skin their knees or fall off the jungle gym. They've cut themselves on our raft after a rough game of push and shove, and in one case we received a hospital bill for the stitches. They complain that the check-out time is too early and try to prove their point by taking an extra long time to leave the grounds as we wait to clean their cabins. And they complain that the check-in time is too late, which they boisterously announce when they show up well before we're ready.

Over the years I've grown more and more strict about our policies, but one area where I have no mercy is the check-in time on Saturday. Our written reservation confirmation practically begs guests not to arrive before 3:30 pm, because their "cabins won't be ready and we're unavailable." Since we have only six hours to get all the cleaning done, eat lunch and then change clothes, we need every minute. But each year, the jerks arrive early and demand attention.

"I just drove all the way from Florida and I think I'm doing pretty good!" said one white-haired, white-Cadillac-driving, bad-grammar-spouting old man one Saturday, who insisted on getting into his cabin at 1:30 pm. Not only was I caught in my cleaning lady attire, which is a capital offense, but also on that day the sofa in the cabin he had reserved was under repair and in six pieces on the living room floor. The cabin needed at least another hour before it was ready.

"People come from all over, sir," I said. "We're simply not ready for check-in. If you read your confirmation guidelines, you'll see that we're not open until 3:30 pm. Why don't you park that Caddie and head down to the beach and enjoy the lake for awhile." Translation? Chill out, old man. I've found that lots of men who are old enough to be my father have treated me like a child instead of a person with whom they are doing business. One once cut into a call on my business line from the pay phone in the recreation cabin and told me to get off the phone.

"How long are you going to be on this phone?" he asked, "I'm trying to make a call in here." I felt like a naughty teenager gabbing to my girlfriend about the cute boy behind me in algebra class, instead of a businesswoman answering questions about Lakeview Lodge for a potential booking.

Another man, who showed up one Saturday just before 3:00 pm and caught me in the office returning videos to the library, knocked hard on the door when he found it locked.

"I'm here for check-in," he said.

"I'll be with you in about fifteen minutes, no more than a half-hour," I said. I would have gladly gotten a little jump-start on my check-in paperwork, which I will do if I'm ready. But in this case, there was still the matter of my final cabin inspection.

"But it's time for check-in," he said, pointing to his watch.

"I can be with you at 3:30," I said.

He reached inside his shirt pocket, pulled out an envelope containing his reservation confirmation and waved it in the air like he was hailing a taxi. "Your confirmation says that check-in time is 3:00."

"I'm sorry," I said. "It's actually 3:30 and I really need just a few more minutes. I'm sure I can get you in even before that."

"It says 3:00!" he insisted.

Of course it read 3:30 and his face dropped when he read it. Even though it was an honest mistake, I marveled at his gall to challenge me on the time. I wondered why he thought that I, the owner of the resort, was unaware of my own policies.

The other reason people are jerks is because they lie. As mentioned before, guests regularly lie about the number of people staying in their cabins, apparently thinking we won't notice when a group of ten is sitting at the beach when they checked in and paid for only six.

Do they think we're stupid?

Imagine the resort as simply being your house and your yard. It's natural to look out the kitchen window when you hear a car pull up. It's natural to want to know who is walking around looking at your garden or the playground where your kids are innocently swinging and climbing. In fact, you make it your business. You guard your property with security cameras and alarm systems, locked gates or even shotguns. (Seeing the bumper sticker, "This property is protected by Smith and Wesson" is not an uncommon experience in the Northwoods.) This is your environment, your home, and you know it well.

It's the people who think we don't notice who is walking around our property at any given time that are stupid! And these stupid people constantly put us in the awkward position of having to approach them with the equivalent of a rulebook in hand. We approach these "strangers" and authoritatively ask, "May I help you?"

"Oh, I'm with Mr. and Mrs. Cabin Five," they say easily. Or worse, they hold up their hands in a halt position and say, "We're fine!" In other words, "We belong here. Please leave us alone." Having just driven past the sign reading, "All Visitors Must Register," they clearly can't be bothered, and I can't stand that. If I have to risk having someone on property mistakenly walk into my kitchen thinking it's the lodge, I sure as hell want to know a little something about them.

As for the guests who've actually registered, we've found clever ways of addressing these stretchers of the truth—these shrinkers of the occupancy levels in their cabins. I think it's called being passive aggressive.

"Excuse me, did you have some extra people show up this week? Do you realize there's an additional charge for people staying overnight? Oh, you didn't know? Well, you can have them come to the office to register and pay the fees any time before five o'clock."

Which brings us to dog owners. We happen to be one of the few Northwoods resorts allowing guests to bring their dogs with them on vacation. Since we were dog owners when we started the business, and we understood the desire to travel with pets and the complications of going on vacation and dealing with leaving pets behind, we decided to make a "pets OK policy." Our policy is pretty strict, in that we only allow a total of two dogs on the property at any given time. They must always be leashed, and never left unattended. We charge a cleaning and damage deposit that's fully refundable, provided there isn't any cleaning or damage due to the dog. Each cabin is equipped with a vacuum cleaner to deal with dog hairs, and we tell our guests with dogs that if we find any evidence of the dog in the cabin, we'll keep the deposit.

It's rare that we keep a dog deposit. Even if dog owners break the rules our history has been that we don't have the nerve to keep their money. We either really like the guests or the dogs didn't actually cause too much trouble. But over the years there have been exceptions that not only make it necessary for us to keep the deposit, but make us to want to ban dogs from the property all together. And the more I get put in the awkward position of having to discipline guests like they're naughty students and I'm Mother Superior, the braver I become about cashing that check.

Take, for example, the first time we had a guest leave his dog in the cabin all day long while he went off to fish. We discovered this disregard for the rules at five o'clock in the morning, which is when he left and when his big golden retriever started complaining about being left alone. A barking, whining dog at that hour is as upsetting to the serenity of the morning as the occasional car alarm that goes off in the middle of the night is to REM sleep. Time after time pet owners insist that their dogs don't bark. "Our dog has not only gone to obedience school, he rarely if ever lets out a bark," they say. (We hear this statement as much as the "you're living my dream life statement.") We also hear "our dogs are our kids," from nearly every pet-owning couple without children. "We never leave them unattended."

People have very different definitions of the word "never." It's as baffling as former President Clinton's statement, "It depends on what the meaning of the word 'is' is."

One very well-behaved dog, who had been on the property several summers in a row, was once left alone in the cabin all afternoon. We might never have discovered this fact if my husband hadn't gone into to the cabin one afternoon to repair a malfunctioning oven. By the way, who in the world bakes a twenty-one pound turkey while on vacation at the lake instead of the usual spaghetti dinners and burgers on the grill? But I digress. Mike knocked on the door and this muscular black lab changed capes from man's best friend to a very protective "Underdog" when he tapped on the door. As the dog heaved his body against the door, digging his toenails into the hardwood floor, his toothy roar came face-to-face with my startled husband, and that momentary scare was definitely worth the thirty-five bucks we took in the form of a damage deposit.

We now have a zero tolerance dog policy.

The worst kind of dog-owning guests are the kind who allow their furry little friends to sleep in bed with them. Again, most owners insist their dog never climbs on furniture of any kind, least of all the bed, and they often mention that the dog always sleeps in a kennel and is more comfortable there. But week after week I find that the Veluxe blankets, you know the thick, velvety kind often found in hotel rooms, are covered with dog hairs. They might as well be called Velcro blankets for the way the hairs stick to them. Cleaning them is not as simple as throwing them in the laundry. Each hair has to be plucked off individually, which can be a very time-consuming chore. I have spare blankets I use to replace the contaminated ones since there simply isn't time on Saturdays to make them good as new; but I growl like a bear whenever I discover that a dog has been sleeping in my bed.

In the summer of 2001, in addition to the damage deposit we started charging for dogs who spent the week. As we had hoped, this helped alleviate the problem of guests bringing dogs without preregistering. Since our policy only allows two dogs on the property, it's vital that guests let us know they wish to bring their dogs, so we know whether or not we can approve. There have been too many instances where we've had three, four, even six dogs show up on Saturday where guests say they either "didn't see" the notation in the confirmation literature, or didn't think the rule applied to them.

When we lived in California, I remember several parks which did not allow dogs, and almost all those that did had leash laws. I recall one park with a big sign reading "All dogs must be on a leash." Below it, someone had scrawled, "Yes, this means YOUR dog." While there isn't a STOP sign in the town of Berkeley that doesn't have a political message painted below the white letters "stop," (stop war, stop rape, stop eating meat, stop driving…) this plea to dog owners stands out in my mind because of the very common trait among dog owners which is that *their* dog isn't in the least bit offensive.

If I hear the sentence, "my dog never barks when I'm away," one more time I'm going to insist on video proof. What I really want to ask is: "HOW DO YOU KNOW IF YOU'RE NOT THERE?"

I sometimes wonder if people realize how transparent they are. Since we opened our pro shop and now experience daily outside traffic for the disc golf course, we've opened ourselves up to a whole new group of liars, er, I mean, customers. One day two young men and a boy came in, and the boy looked young enough to be under twelve, thereby falling into the free green fee category. Our green fee is a very reasonable four dollars for all day play, which includes the use of golf discs. We do not charge for children under twelve, as we're continually trying to introduce kids to the game and keep it an inexpensive family activity. In any event, when I asked the boy how old he was, his face went blank. He stared back at me as if I had just asked him to explain the theory of relativity.

"Your age, please?" I asked again in my best Mother Superior voice. Still no response. Asking a kid his age is like asking his name, or what my daughter's first grade teacher calls a sight-word. She says that the six and seven year olds in her class "should be able to look at a required list of words on a page and say them out loud without hesitation." You expect an immediate response.

"Don't you know how old you are?" I asked with blatant sarcasm lacing my personal set of sight-words.

He still didn't answer me, but instead, looked to one of his escorts for help.

"Uh, he's eleven," said one of the older fellas.

Of course I knew three seconds earlier that I was about to be the victim of a bullshit, four-dollar lie, but I let him/them get away with it, saying, "I should charge you just because you DON'T know how old you are."

A few bad apples come around every summer. Mike's response to this story was to suggest we do away with the under-twelve-free rule. If they're going to lie to us and put us in yet another awkward position, screw it. But at least someone in his group paid a green fee. We've had many disc golf cases of "dine and dash" over the years, where people come and play the course and feel that the green fee doesn't apply to them. This mentality is understandable since most disc golf courses are located in public parks and are free to play. Many, many times we've been faced with the question of why we charge to play our course. Our answer is simple. "The equipment alone cost us in excess of $10,000."

That usually shuts them up.

One disc golfer came in during the off-season, just after we had our black top road sealed. The contractors hadn't yet finished the job and had barricaded the front entrance. Imagine their surprise when an eighteen-year-old kid came barreling down the road in a green Honda, leaving tire tracks like big black ribbons etched into the tar. They confronted the kid and showed him an alternate way out, so they could repair the damage and he wouldn't wreck that too when leaving. But, of course, the kid was of the jerk variety, and in spite of their warning and instructions, he drove over the fresh sealant again. Luckily, the contractors got the license plate of the Honda, and our local DA deemed this kind of reckless behavior of a "criminal nature." We pressed charges.

The previous owners made it no secret that they were chased out of the business because they were "sick of people wrecking their stuff." After a decade of dealing with the jerks, we're sick of it, too. But I guess you can say we've learned to fight back.

Staff Infection

When I traveled through Kenya with my sister, we experienced a wide range of accommodations. Each place we stayed, however, no matter how simple or elaborate, was lousy with staff. Spotting an actual property owner in some places was about as rare as finding an albino rhino in the wild. In most cases, property owners were white or British, which is the name by which Caucasian people are referred. Some were of Indian descent, or Asian. And in all cases the staff consisted entirely of Africans—or black-skinned people of tribes varying according to region.

On an island in north central Kenya we spent about four days at a quaint, outdoor facility called Island Camp. To get there we rode north from Mt. Kenya in the back seat of an old Land Rover. At the wheel was a Kikuyu man named Stanley.

After a long, dusty journey, Stanley dropped us at a landing where we boarded a twenty-foot banana boat that plunged through the hippo and crocodile-invested waters of Lake Barringo and to a small, isolated sanctuary.

Greeting us at the shore were the camp managers, a young British couple. Judging by their warm welcome, they were delighted to have us. "Welcome *wgani*," they said with broad smiles and soft British accents. *Wgani* is "guests" in Swahili.

Their names were Hugo and Antionette. They were married only a year, and were new at managing Island Camp. We were their first guests and they practically hugged us as they helped us off the boat.

"Do you realize you're famous?" Hugo asked. "I hope you have a copy of today's newspaper. We made the front page. There's a headline three inches thick!"

Hugo explained that there had been a bitter fight for the ownership of this island resort, which was finally resolved by our appearance as first guests of the new management. He said his family had built the tented camp over twenty years earlier, and managed the operation from the start. Then three years prior to our banana boat arrival, the management was handed over to a large hotel company and, according to Hugo, they let it go "absolutely to pieces." So, in stepped none other than the son of Kenya's president, who decided he wanted the camp and claimed it as his own by illegally signing over the lease to himself. They said he had never even seen the property, but had heard good things.

Island Camp, for my sister and me, was a magical place. From Tent #27, perched atop a steep, rocky cliff, we looked out over the rusty, alkaline waters of Lake Barringo, a lake with the permanent color of sunset. A steady tropical breeze kept the otherwise hot air temperature quite comfortable. And color, vibrant rich color was everywhere in the form of bougainvillea, golden shower and bird of paradise plants. Florescent lizards, butterflies and birds darted back and forth across the dirt paths and the crystal sky. There were no roads and therefore no motorized vehicles, but goats roamed freely and one day I found one on the grass roof of our tent. Inside the tent our side-by-side single beds were protected by mosquito nets, and we were well cared for by several staff members. One man brought us tea in the morning, another fresh towels; another kept us informed of the day's schedule of meals and activities. Everything was new to me and I felt like I was a child experiencing YMCA camp for the first time. This place was paradise. No wonder people were fighting over it.

Lease disputes in Kenya are not uncommon. Since independence from Great Britain and fledgling, corrupt governments took hold; residents witnessed a great deal of change. While almost every white person one meets in the country is still in a position of relative wealth and stature, owning businesses and land, in particular, puts them in a precarious and unstable position. Hugo informed us that his mother, the manager of a farm near the town of Molo, had been recently caught in another lease dispute and was literally burned out of her home.

"She's staying there to hold her ground," said Hugo. "But she's living in a burned out building with broken windows and two armed *askaries* (guards)." Because of what happened to his mother, Hugo and his wife decided to fight for the right to re-attain the lease to Island Camp, and acquire all the licenses required to maintain charge. In the years before the takeover, their agreement with the local inhabitants and the tribal chief of the island had been verbal. The situation worked because the camp provided some sixty staff positions. Also, a percentage of the profits went directly to the island population to build schools and medical facilities. When the president's son took over, however, he did so with complete disregard for the both the island inhabitants and Hugo's family. All the employees were suddenly laid-off because the camp, renamed "Island Bed Camp," was to be completely refurbished. He wanted to add more tents to make more money and it was predicted that he would, in turn, completely alter or even destroy the serenity offered by the rather prehistoric surroundings there.

Obviously, Hugo's fight was successful and it had become his and Antionette's turn to give it a go. I appreciated their newness and enthusiasm. Their youth gave the whole experience a fresh feel. I'll never forget the warmth of their initial welcome, and when I first became a resort owner I hoped to be able to make each one of our guests feel as special as they made us feel.

Like every other place we stayed while on our African safari, everything here seemed to run smoothly. I think it had a lot to do with the staff and the plentiful number of employees. Historically an agrarian culture, Kenya has seen a population swell and a dwindling of farmable land, making tourism a mainstay of the Kenyan economy. Local tribal people hold every job from cook to naturalist, houseboy to groundskeeper. And as Hugo and

Antionette explained to us over dinner one evening, there's a lot going on behind the scenes that guests of their facility never see.

"For example," said Antionette, who had joined us for coffee one evening after a delay in the kitchen, "the other night there was a problem with one of the blokes who was brutally beaten. Someone handed a note to me about noon yesterday, which simply reported the incident and said, 'to Kabernet hospital.'" She assumed from the note that he had been checked out at the local clinic but probably needed x-rays or perhaps additional care, so he was sent to the mainland hospital.

This was indeed the case, but not the reason she was detained.

Antionette was detained in the kitchen because of a confrontation with other staff members over the incident. They accused her of not caring about the man's wounds since she herself didn't arrange to have him boated to the mainland. But she had only learned of the beating after he had already left the island.

"It's fairly common for staff to put off telling those in charge about their problems—be it their parents, teachers or employers," said Antionette. "They're so afraid of getting in trouble or, worse, beaten. It's just difficult having the responsibility of a staff. All of their problems and squabbles become your business."

No kidding.

Anyone running a small business knows that good employees are hard to find. This is one reason why a mom-and-pop operation appealed to us. If we could do everything ourselves, staff wouldn't be an issue. But as Sandy Point grew in size and our little family began to grow, it became necessary to hire help.

Aside from the teenage girl I hired to help clean the cabins on Saturdays, in 1995 we decided to find someone to thoroughly clean our home once a week. It no longer made sense that I was busy cleaning cabins for the guests but, in the meantime our house was always trashed. The term "busman's holiday" came to mind every time I changed the sheets on our beds or scrubbed our toilets, and I dreaded the chores. Besides, I was pregnant and spending a lot of time off my feet. I didn't feel like doing much of anything between the frequent trips to the bathroom.

The first cleaning lady (hired through an agency that charged us twelve dollars an hour) lasted only three weeks. Cleaning obviously wasn't a profession for her—just something to do to get the bills paid between jobs. She turned up her nose in disgust each time she entered an unclean room. I told her from the start that I wasn't the type of person who "cleaned up before the cleaning lady came," and I'm sure she wished that I had.

A young woman who lasted about the same length of time replaced her, although it seemed like she was in our house a lot longer. To this day there's a green enamel paint stain on the carpet in our bedroom from where she spilled wash water once, after filling a paint bucket with suds to clean the bathroom.

"Just to let you know," she said with one foot out the door, "I stained your rug."

This girl was partially responsible for teaching me the importance of keeping my distance from the hired help. I didn't hire them to come into my house to have a chat over coffee, but rather, to clean my toilets while I drank a cup of coffee in the other room. There were plenty of guests outside on the grounds with whom I could share stories and socialize and they, in fact, paid me to do so. But this one, who was probably about ten or twelve years younger than I, was a single mother who took the job to try to earn enough money to regain custody of her children who had become wards of the state. Normally I would applaud anyone who made an honest effort to earn a decent living and do right by her children, but she was an absolute puzzle.

"My kids are nothin' but brats," she often said. "I can't stand being around them." And then, placing her hand on my basketball-sized belly she said, "You just wait. First they come out all cute and you love 'em right up. But I'm tellin' ya, they grow up and become brats."

When she quit, the agency said they couldn't find anyone else to do the job. They were the only cleaning operation in the area, and it was hard finding employees to last longer than three or four weeks. "In a resort community where there are so many seasonal cleaning jobs, all the good ones are taken," they said, matter-of-fact like.

Luckily we found a "good one" by checking the community bulletin board at the local grocery store. She had placed an index card with her name and phone number and Mike called her to see if she would take the job of cleaning our house. She lasted five years before she moved to another town. After a year or so of cleaning our house, she joined the Saturday cleaning staff and helped make the job fun. This gal truly loved to clean. She did it well and she did it happily.

We paid her well, rewarded her with bonuses, gave her a car to use and, at one point, allowed her to move into our home. We even introduced her to a disc golf player who liked to spend time at our resort, who ended up taking her away from us to live with him.

After she rode off into the sunset we hired a pair of sloppy sisters who charged far too much and did a mediocre job. They stayed on for a while, until one day they just didn't show up. A half-hour after they were expected, and our stripped beds sat waiting for new sheets, sister number one called to say that our kind of cleaning wasn't the kind of cleaning they wanted to do anymore. Our dirt was just no longer good enough for them. Apparently, in their eyes *we* were the sloppy ones. (They were right. We are sloppy. That's why we hired them.) But we've been doing our own house cleaning since that day.

One employee Mike hired to help with the grounds work was a vagrant who ambled in one day looking for work. He had us quoting a *Saturday Night Live* skit every time we spoke about him because he was literally the "man who lived in a van down by the river." The good news was that he always worked hard when he was on the property. But the bad news was he scared the guests. He had long, uncombed hair and three, maybe four teeth.

I'm Living Your Dream Life

He lurked on the hillside overlooking the lake, silently trimming and raking, and for all anyone knew harbored a chain saw and might turn it on any one of us at any time. Of the ten days or so that he worked for us, a few times he brought his van to our property and his wife and children spent the day deep in the woods, never venturing out into the sunlight. And then one day he was just gone.

Another employee was a high school kid whose name escapes me. He was from the high school work program, and was hired to work during school hours from Monday through Friday. His only job was to cut and clear brush in a swampy area by the lake. On day four of his tenure he asked for his paycheck a day early because he needed to buy groceries for his family—or something like that. Mike paid him for the hours he put in and we never saw him again. The site remains uncleared to this day.

And then along came an enterprising seventeen-year-old kid who, encouraged by his father, called several area resorts looking for work. He stayed on board and did a great job for over seven years. But then some NHL hockey player moved to town and offered him twenty bucks an hour to sit at his home and wait for deliveries, so doing real labor for half that wage was no longer attractive to him. Who could blame the guy?

One summer there was a college kid who sought a job at our resort because his major was hotel management and his hobby was disc golf. He was a likeable, good-looking kid and we hired him as a summer intern and let him live at the Resort. So, in exchange for room and board and an hourly wage, he raked the beach, mowed the lawns and tended to the disc golf course.

We loved this boy and treated him like family. He was quiet, hard working and really seemed to like us and like the work. When it was time to go back to school, we were sorry to see him go.

The next summer he graduated and found a job in our community. He asked if he could live at the resort again in exchange for working evenings and weekends at the property, or about twenty hours a week. He assured us he could fit it all into his schedule, and we were delighted to have him back.

But then he met a girl and his priorities changed. Again, who could blame the guy?

As the weeks passed, he no longer spent his evenings and days off working for us. He spent them working *on* her. Since she lived in another town, commuting for romance took up a lot of time. And when she came to the resort and spent long weekends parading around the lakefront in her bikini and using all our facilities while he worked some place else, she developed the distinct flavor of an uninvited houseguest.

What I learned that summer was that just as you can choose your spouse but not your in-laws, you can choose your employees but not their lovers. The issue of a girlfriend never entered my mind.

Eventually the young, smitten man came to me and said we needed to talk.

"I think twenty hours a week is too much to ask of me in exchange for free rent."

"But you're not giving us any time at all," I said. "And when you are around the resort, you're so distracted or tired or something you're causing more damage than anything else."

It was true. Suddenly everything was broken, misplaced or done in a way that was far from satisfactory. He backed our truck into a telephone pole, drove a nail through a water pipe in the bathroom of his apartment, and ran over the expensive hose nozzle—not the cheap one. He mowed down a bed of perennials that were just about to bloom, and backed up a car to our house in order to load something and left muddy tire ruts six inches deep on either side of the walkway, again wiping out flowerbeds. And these are just the few things I can remember. I told him he only had to work ten hours a week, and then he again came to me and said even that was asking too much. So we suggested he look for a new place to live.

Employees come in all shapes and sizes. Some stay for short stints, others stay on board for a while longer. Really, as I see it, getting a good one has a lot to do with good luck. But after a few years in this business, we're getting better about guessing who is going to work out and who isn't. You can't help but make mistakes in hiring because they all put on their best faces when they're trying to get the job. Just the other day we read in the paper that a young man (who worked the grounds for us for a while) was recently put in jail for statutory rape. So, you must learn to be extremely intuitive, and by all means check references and don't ignore gut instincts.

The way one feels about employees is one issue, but the way they feel about you can become your biggest headache. I read a statistic in the paper a few years ago regarding employee attitudes toward their employers. This stat indicated that a whopping ninety percent of workers under the age of thirty-five believe their bosses are ripping them off.

I think I can understand why.

First of all we're talking about workers under the age of thirty-five, which makes it an issue of maturity. In many cases it means the Generation called X, or children of baby boomers. I'm not sure exactly what happened to this group, but I do know that many of the Gen Xer's I've met really don't want to work. And those who do work believe they should be in top positions with high salaries without the benefit of experience. Simply put, they don't understand the magnitude of responsibility that owning a business entails.

Employees tend to only see everything the business owner has. They see the money come in, but they don't see it go out. They see the property but don't see the property taxes or the mortgage. They see the buildings but don't see the insurance bills. They see the lights but not the electrical bills; feel the warmth but not the ever-increasing expense of the propane bills. And, of course, they have no concept of self-employment tax, commercial liability policies, or paying for health insurance. They have no vested interest in whether your business survives or fails, as they believe they can always move on to another job that pays more and requires fewer responsibilities.

A mom-and-pop-operation can survive beautifully if mom and pop are the only workers and can handle all the chores. But when mom and pop have a couple of babies and decide that the winters in Wisconsin are too long and too cold, and like snowbirds decide to fly south for the winter, the operation can suffer. If you try to hire a replacement mom and pop, look out.

I include the following information on our experiences with staff for anyone reading who is seriously considering the business of resort owner-ship or inn-keeping in a seasonal climate, or hiring another couple or a caretaker to run your business, whatever it may be.

After our first few years in the woods we decided to move to Tucson, Arizona. Let's face it, winter in the Northwoods isn't for everyone. This is the Snow Belt. And in the Snow Belt, sometimes the snow starts falling in September and doesn't stop until April. The lake freezes solid—so solid you can drive your truck out to the middle—and one year it didn't melt until mid-May. For weeks at a time double-digit sub-zero temperatures are normal, and the term "cabin fever" becomes a condition rather than a term. This is one reason why there are so many Green Bay Packer fans in the state of Wisconsin. There's not a whole lot more to do on cold winter weekends than stay inside somewhere in front of a football game.

Before the kids came we handled it rather well. It was a cozy little hon-eymoon filled with cross-country skiing during the day and Scrabble games next to the fire at night. But the babies changed everything. Getting our toddler dressed in boots and a snowsuit was an arduous chore, especially when as soon as you got her outside she wanted to go back inside. And some days it was just too cold and, therefore, dangerous to have her out-side.

Isolation was another issue. Like papa, mama and baby bear alone in the woods, only the occasional lost Goldilocks showed up on the property riding a snow mobile and looking for directions. The winter guests only came on weekends and most of them didn't consist of families with young children. Our nearest neighbors were too far for daily visits, and we didn't much care to visit them anyway, especially after the Lakeview Lodge rezoning issue. Play dates and neighborhood games of tag and foursquare just didn't exist. Alas, I had no Wilma Flintstone next door, Mike had no Fred, and Willow had no Pebbles. Isolation may be fine for a young married couple in love, but not for a family. Families need other families to help keep them sane.

The issue of schooling arose as well. When we moved to the Northwoods B.C. (Before Children) we didn't think to check out the public school in our district. And this is something we did wrong. In our haste to get out of the city and develop our disc golf resort, our business plan didn't include the very personal issue of raising children.

I knew I wanted to have a baby, but I didn't know the first thing about raising it.

We knew there was a public school in our area, understood it was brand new, and that seemed good enough. The school was a beautiful new facility and was located on the Indian Reservation near our property. At first we thought that was great, since cultural diversity was important to us. And compared to where we came from in California, there wasn't a whole lot of diversity in the Northwoods. Having friends of different cultures was something we liked about our life and missed in our new home. But it turned out this school was not a place where we wanted to have our children educated, and there was little if any choice for private schooling nearby. After our daughter was born, people asked us where we planned to send her to school. Usually the question was, "You're not going to send her to that awful Flambeau school are you?"

"What do you mean? Isn't it a good school?"

"Not if you're a white kid it isn't. The white kids get beat up on a daily basis."

While I didn't want to believe this, I couldn't find anyone to deny it was the case. Several parents confirmed it. Teachers confirmed it, too. And Mike,

145

who drove a school bus on the reservation during our first few winters in Wisconsin saw first-hand incidents of both abuse and neglect, and discipline issues arose daily. He saw kids run out of the house in the morning on cold winter days without jackets, and parents were often not at the bus stop to meet their kids when they were scheduled for a drop-off. One physical education teacher I knew who worked at the school said she spent half an hour of each class period with discipline issues rather than her lesson plan. But we still believed our daughter would survive. We were willing to give the school a chance.

But then one day at the town hall, a woman told me her child attended that school and was beaten up nearly once a week. When I asked why, she said it was because her son was white.

"How can you stand to watch your child suffer like that?" I asked.

"Well, I think it's a rough world out there no matter who you are or where you go. Sure, I'd prefer it if my kid didn't come home with a black eye, but I think the sooner he learns that the world can be cruel the better he'll turn out."

Fine for her, but that wasn't a lesson we wanted to teach our children. From that moment forward I knew my flaxen-haired, blue-eyed daughter would not attend school there. In the spring of 2002, I read a series of Letters to the Editor in the local newspaper supporting the school and complementing the great educational strides of the curriculum. Most were in defense of an administration accused of sexual harassment against a staff member. When the charges were dropped the subject became cold-weather fodder for newspaper readers. As a reader who happens to spend thousands of dollars in taxes to support this school, I was pleased to finally receive some positive feedback regarding this learning facility.

When we chose Tucson as our nesting place we made the school district a top priority and, in effect, got a double reward: A mild winter climate and a place where we felt comfortable sending our children. But we also found ourselves with the task of finding an adequate caretaker for the winter season. With the addition of our year-round units, we had built-up a winter business and hoped it would continue to grow and be profitable.

Since the first winter we became snowbirds, each year the decision hangs over us as to whether or not we're going to close the resort for the winter. Unlike summer guests who book a year in advance, winter guests wait until the snow falls before calling for reservations. So, we rarely have advanced bookings. With the success of the winter business completely reliant on how much snow hits the area—not to mention the unpredictable cost of propane, which we use to heat the cabins—it's impossible to guess whether or not keeping the cabins open will be worth the effort. Just to cite an example of the propane expense, in 1999 we paid a total of $4,500 for propane. Without any foresight or warning that expense jumped to $9,700 the following year. Due to propane expenses alone we barely broke even that winter. Luckily the caretakers that year did a decent job and we didn't have much to worry about, knowing the resort was left in capable hands. Expenses and natural resources are something one always has to deal with and sometimes it just takes a little juggling with the budget to keep things afloat. But when dealing with human resources—read employees—a good one is worth twice the value of utility expenses. But a bad one? Ugh! The stories I could tell. We've considered giving up the yo-yo lifestyle but after one winter in Tucson, the closest thing to paradise either of us has experienced in a hometown, we were ready for more.

Being away from the resort for several months enables us to refuel and face the busiest part of the year with enthusiasm instead of burnout. Before our kids were in school we had the perfect lifestyle—six months per year in each place. We left behind both the bitter cold of the Northwoods and the hellish heat of the Sonoran desert with each move. Interestingly, the year after we made a go of this snowbird thing (based solely on our children's educational needs) Wisconsin passed a measure for school choice, allowing children to apply for admission into other district schools tuition free. Since there were now two good schools from which to choose, we suddenly had to admit we were winter wimps who only fled to the desert for the climate.

But it was more than just climate. In Tucson we've got neighbors. Neighbors we actually like and who like us. Willow found a best friend instantly. She lives down the street and they are the same age. When they came together for the first time they draped their arms around each other and, I swear, there are no two children on the planet who play together as beautifully as these two. And it just so happens her mother is the Wilma Flintstone I was looking for, and her husband the water buffalo lodge, er, golf partner my husband found for himself.

So, in order to keep this lifestyle we've designed, we've forced ourselves to deal with the issue of winter caretakers. And we've had both good and bad luck with the series of caretakers we've hired to do the job.

In our experience it's better to hire someone with an independent contractor status rather than take him on as an employee. And by all means we'll never again set up a so-called profit-sharing system, especially when the business isn't technically making a profit. (As mentioned earlier, employees will almost always believe that you're making more money than you really are.) Independent contractors take care of their own social security and self-employment taxes and generally have their own insurance. It saves me from having to submit monthly payroll tax reports and getting involved with their personal lives any more than I already have to by bringing them into our business and, consequently, our life.

By hiring an independent contractor, we have a signed contract in hand outlining the terms of the job. Not only does the caretaker have a complete job description, but also, a time frame indicating start and end dates of the job. One winter our caretaker decided the brutal Northwoods winter wasn't what he wanted after all, and decided to take another job in another city. He moved out around March 1st. The worst part about this was that he told us in January and then with a newfound lame-duck status, stopped doing the job. For the next six weeks our phone rang with complaint after complaint from guests about how they were treated or from people who had stopped by the resort looking for future accommodations, who were basically told to get lost. When the money came up short due to his decision to give away the use of a cabin to a family member over a holiday weekend, and he expected to be paid according to the terms of the original contract, well, it was not a pretty scene.

Currently, we're blessed with a wonderful winter caretaker who in the summer works as a full-time maintenance man and disc golf course pro. What's special about this man is that of all the people who have worked for us over the years, he's the first to really care about Sandy Point Resort as a business. He takes his job very seriously and it shows in everything he does.

Here's an important note: If you're going to hire anyone, be sure—absolutely sure—to check references of former employers. I even recommend you ask the important question, "Did he or she care about the work?" During the interview process ask them again and again if they truly grasp the reality of the position. If you're unsure whether or not they understand the role of winter caretaker in Snow Belt, sit them down in front of the movie based on the Stephen King novel *The Shining*. If they show the slightest bit of empathy for the Jack Nicholson character, do yourself a favor and send them packing.

There are far too many workers out there who only take jobs to fill time or to live what they perceive to be *your* dream life. We made the mistake of letting some of our caretakers move into our house and, in effect, take over our life as well as our business. It's a big mistake. After the first few winters of coming home to a redecorated space where all my refrigerator magnets, photos, newspaper clippings and birth announcements had been removed and left in a neat pile on the nightstand next to my bed, this mama bear decided she didn't want anyone else sitting in my chair, eating my porridge or sleeping in my bed. So we arranged separate living quarters for the staff and it has made a world of difference for them and us.

Also, avoid having any work done on the property when you're not there and the caretaker is left to oversee the project. One winter when one of our cabins was under construction, our caretaker kept turning off the electricity and the workers couldn't operate their power tools. She was convinced that the outdoor security light was burning up too much electricity and the cost was somehow cutting into "her profits." In the morning when the workers arrived bright and early at 7:00 am, they couldn't operate their tools because she hadn't yet gotten out of bed to switch on the circuit breaker. Another winter we had a building re-roofed, and a different caretaker kept calling us to say the job was going too slowly and that if we had hired him to do the job, it would have taken half the time and we would have gotten twice the quality.

Another winter when a couple was in the position, I dealt primarily with the woman. Whenever there was a problem—and there happened to be a lot of problems that winter—I called her and did my best to work out solutions. At the time I actually believed each conversation ended on a positive note. But I was an idiot for believing that. What I didn't know was that the conversation continued in Wisconsin long after I had hung up in Arizona.

It's called pillow talk and it's why you should avoid hiring a couple.

It wasn't long before I received a nasty phone call from her husband who accused me of telling his wife to "change her personality."

For the record, I never told her to change her personality.

More than once we were accused mid-way through the winter of not paying enough money for the "incredibly difficult" job at hand. When I reminded one of the disgruntled caretakers that in addition to paying an hourly wage for cleaning cabins and working the grounds, we paid the utility expenses and provided rent-free facilities in a big, beautiful house, he practically spit at me through the phone, saying free rent didn't mean anything.

"You'd have to pay your mortgage anyway," he hissed.

This taught me to always declare the monetary value for living quarters and include it in the contract as a benefit. This may seem like a trivial detail, but believe me, when it has a price tag on it, it's easier for everyone to read.

When it comes to hiring, in general, we try to not make the same mistakes twice. In fact that's a sort of business philosophy for us. When we were new to the resort business, we had to give ourselves room to make mistakes. The point is to learn from them and simply make new mistakes instead of doing the same thing wrong again and again. But sometimes old mistakes disguise themselves as new ones and before you know it, you find yourself in a familiar situation that has you scratching your head and saying things like, "been there, done that."

Due to dread, apprehension, laziness, whatever you want to call it, we have never advertised for the position of winter caretaker. Certainly it was easier to believe that we wouldn't find anyone right for the job than to actually search. Each of the many caretakers we've hired over the years have all come to us asking—and in one case, begging—for the job. Prior to our current caretaker, the only person to last more than one season was a woman who I will call Darla.

This is not her real name, but I choose to call her Darla because she was, well, a darling person. Darla, who was almost my age and couldn't believe it the day my father, while visiting, blurted out my life history and informed her that I was older than she thought, started a cleaning business because she believed it would be less stressful than her previous job as a day care worker. She was married, in her mid-thirties and childless.

"My husband's sterile," she announced the day we met her. "And I want a baby. I figure I can make enough money by cleaning to pay for in vitro fertilization." More information than we cared to know during the interview, but you had to applaud her honesty and her effort.

One thing we immediately liked about her was that she clearly wanted to work as a cleaning lady. Darla began by scouring our home on a weekly basis. She always showed up and always did a fabulous job. Really, a fabulous job. Here was the world's most gifted cleaning woman. Each week she did the standard stuff but never failed to add a special touch like cleaning and organizing a junk drawer or rearranging a linen closet with towels folded so neatly you didn't want to use them. She alphabetized the kids' bookshelves, displayed their stuffed animals and brought them presents every week. Darla was happy in her work. She burst into the house with curls bouncing, sweat on her brow and a big plastic bottle of Mountain Dew in her hand and worked at a feverish pace, chattering joyously the whole time.

We loved her.

Soon she joined the Saturday cleaning staff and exhibited even higher standards of excellence than I. I'd look at my watch and think "good enough" while she stood up on a chair to get one last cob web off a log beam or one stubborn spill completely removed from the oven pan. She even found a friend to come on board the year after the teenagers left the cleaning staff, and it was a welcome change to work with mature women who actually cared about getting the cabins cleaned.

While she looked on as I went through a second pregnancy, unfortunately for Darla, the in vitro didn't take. She never moped about it in front of us or hinted at feelings of jealously or wantonness as we welcomed a second healthy daughter to our family. Whatever sadness she may have felt was overshadowed by her zealous energy. This was a woman who was meant to have a child. She possessed every motherly instinct known to woman and yet no baby to rock to the soporose tick-tock of her biological clock.

Then her marriage failed, too. Because she rarely spoke negatively about her husband, we were surprised when she gave us the news. They parted on good terms, however, and continued to share their house until it was sold. And considering the caretaker position at the resort, Darla presented herself as an applicant.

"Well, you know I can clean," she said. "And I know these cabins inside out."

"That's true," we said. "But how do you feel about living all the way out here all alone for the winter?"

"I'm a Northwoods girl," she said heartily. "I've friends I can call if I get in trouble. But I'm sure I'll be okay."

And okay she was. More than okay. Darla did a wonderful job. She enabled us to spend a very peaceful winter in Tucson and rarely called with any problems or concerns. She either handled things herself or found someone else who could handle things for her. And the best part is that she restored our confidence in hiring. We found trust again, in her and in ourselves. Not wanting to make the same mistakes we made with previous caretakers, we threw out the misnamed profit sharing contract idea we had used originally, and hired her as an employee with an hourly wage complete with deductions like social security. We paid her electricity and trash bills and she paid her propane, telephone and premium satellite TV bills. And in addition to free rent, we offered Darla the use of our four-wheel drive sport utility vehicle. She drove an older compact car that was fine for driving around town, but living out in the woods during the winter required four-wheel drive. We drew up an agreement separate from the caretaker contract, which said the vehicle was for her personal use and to be used only when necessary. To make sure it wasn't overused we allotted her 1,000 miles a month. Any additional miles would cost her something like a quarter a mile.

"Are you sure you want to give her the car, too?" asked more than one family member and a few curious friends. "Don't you think that's a little much?"

"She's going to do a lot of little things around the resort that don't figure into her hourly wage," we answered. "We're paying her to clean but not sit around and read or watch TV while she waits for guests to show up. So it's kind of a trade for that gray area of responsibility. Besides, we feel more comfortable knowing she's got reliable transportation."

"What about the truck with the snow plow?"

"We hired a service."

"Didn't you guys learn anything through that accident where you got sued because someone was driving your boat?"

Good question. But Darla was covered on our insurance policy. Our agreement was that if anything happened she'd have to pay for the damages.

But nothing happened. At least not during the first winter.

Darla asked to stay with us through the summer and committed to the next winter season. Because this meant she would continue living in our house during the summer, Mike was pretty reluctant about this. He didn't want a roommate. Frankly, neither did I, but I wasn't reluctant to continue employing Darla. I thought it meant that I'd have a lot more help around the house and with the kids. Having her stay meant that he'd have to make a priority of finishing the lower level apartment on our house, so she would have her own living quarters with her own entrance. Temporarily she stayed in our guest room, located on the main floor.

Darla continued to clean our house one day a week, and helped clean cabins on Saturdays. She continued to do a marvelous job. But that was it. Extra help with the kids and the house was not something she offered. On her days off she liked to sleep in. And while we were all up with the sun and the loud alarm of the Northwoods that sings every morning in the form of bird calls, the mere idea of someone snoozing in the back bedroom wore on us like a pair of jeans that had gotten too tight. It had been well over a decade since Mike or I had had roommates besides each other and when you live with a spouse, there's just an understanding about lifestyles and habits. You take them "for better or for worse." But when a veritable stranger enters your world after you've attained a certain comfort-level in your life, things like the smell of pungent, lily of the valley perfume wafting in your hallways can actually make you physically sick.

Our incentive to finish the lower level apartment became great, and halfway into the summer we helped her move her beautiful antique furniture into a new space with her own entry to and from the outside world. We were sure that she was happier down there, too. In fairness there's no doubt she had her own objections to *our* habits and lifestyle. A single woman without kids might as well call up Rod Serling and enter the *Twilight Zone*, for how different a place it can be from the world of sleeping in, uninterrupted bathroom time and quiet early evening reading. While it was perfectly normal for us to deal with screaming kids refusing to eat the food in front of them, spilling anything liquid that came within reach, leaving toys and books and shoes and socks and blankets and playing cards in their wakes like Hansel and Gretel's bread crumbs, for a cleaning lady, in particular, it was probably like living in a dumpster.

Childless women, especially those who want children, can be perfect mothers from the outside looking in. When you add years of day care experience, unsolicited advice comes even more often. The truth is most of Darla's advice was good. She loved our girls and her advice was from the heart. Actually, I was interested in whatever anyone could tell me about things like potty-training and thumb-sucking. When my mother was still alive, any time I called her about a problem I had with one of the girls she laughed at me. I still feel her laughing at me when I struggle with the kids in a "you deserve it" kind of way.

Nevertheless, I didn't like being on display in my own home. It was hard enough acting the role of resort owner and having people ask me a zillion questions each time I stepped outside, as if I wore a t-shirt that said "come talk to me and ask me questions about my life." Back then I still had some pride and hadn't yet learned to let go of the luxury called privacy. If and when I lost my temper, I didn't need anyone else to know the real bitch behind the office door. If I poured a second glass of wine before dinner or talked on the phone to my sister for an hour or let the laundry pile up to the rafters or hid out in the bathroom until I finished the Sunday crossword puzzle, it wasn't anyone's business.

This brings up some very important issues. As a resort owner, I am constantly on display. It's time in the spotlight on a very localized platform, but a platform nonetheless. While I have always enjoyed conversations with people and obviously, by writing this book and in my former occupation as a newspaper columnist, discussing my life comes naturally. But everyone needs a little down time. For those of you who have children and know the effect that parenthood has on private moments, guests and employees at your establishment can be looked upon in the same manner. They can be needy, overly inquisitive and, in spite of the office hours you may set, there will always be some who believe their questions certainly aren't an imposition. Employees in particular, constantly look to their employers for answers. And I'm expected to know all the answers and set the perfect example.

If you can't stomach the idea of non-family members rummaging through your property, showing up on your doorstep at all hours and asking you very personal questions on a daily basis, inn-keeping as an occupation is not a good idea for you. One of the benefits of owning a resort with housekeeping units as opposed to a bed and breakfast is that we don't have to feed people and we have separate living quarters from the guests. A friend who once owned a bed-and-breakfast told me of a guest who not only took it upon herself to do all her laundry in the owner's private work area, but also wandered into her bedroom on a self-guided tour of the inn. You must be prepared to share even the most personal moments.

Take, for example, the summer my mother died. It was sudden and, of course, it was awful. My sister, Mary Beth, happened to be visiting that week in mid-July, and we were in town shopping when my husband called on the cell phone with the news that she had suffered a severe stroke. It wasn't her first stroke but it was the "big one"—as our other sister the doctor termed it—and it rendered her brain-dead. She was eighty-years-old and it happened while she was attempting to water-ski—yes, water-ski—an activity she loved and indulged in nearly every summer morning. My five-foot nothing, eighty-five-pound Mom was something of a phenomenon in the retirement community where she and our Dad had lived in Missouri. Skiing didn't cause the stroke, however, as she was merely in the water preparing to take off when it hit. Our Dad said that her last words before the lights went out were, "I think I'm going to drown." He pulled her from the water—the old wooden ski still attached to her foot—and with the help of two kind and caring neighbors named Stan and Ruby, performed CPR until the ambulance arrived. She was airlifted to a hospital in St. Louis where she remained on life-support until my four siblings and I arrived to say good-bye.

It happened on a Monday, which gave me plenty of time before the Saturday turnover to prepare to leave the resort and feel confident that the guest transition would go smoothly. While my sister and I took off for Missouri that night, Mike stayed behind to work with Darla until Sunday. Then he made the twelve-hour drive south for my mother's funeral. We knew we had left the resort (as well as our daughters) in Darla's capable hands. I will always be grateful to Darla for her comfort during that time.

My Mom's death rocked my world. While Mike's mother had passed away thirteen years earlier and happened when we had only begun dating, I witnessed his devastation and the ensuing depression that seemed to last for years; however, I was still terribly shocked by the experience of losing my own mother. She often told me that from the time I was a small child I commented about how fast my life was going. There are times when I still move to pick up the telephone to call and tell her something, including the fact that I lost her far too soon.

When we came home from the funeral everything at the resort looked different. That mystical haze that sometimes hovers over the lake in the early morning seemed to surround every tree, every building and every person I encountered throughout the day. I needed time to stand still for a while and allow me to grieve but, alas, it did not. Instead, time went marching on, indifferent to my needs.

Three weeks later one of my dearest friends got married in Colorado.

She had been a roommate in college and we're as close as sisters. She had honored our friendship by asking me to read at her wedding, which took place outdoors where we were surrounded by mountains, good music and lots of old friends. It was like a college reunion and the perfect time to be with these supportive and caring people. When we had first received the invitation I wanted to put my hands around the bride's neck, since it was an event not to be missed and it took place smack dab in the middle of our busy season and on a Saturday, no less. So, in addition to making the necessary travel and child care arrangements, we faced the task of finding extra help to cover the turnover.

We took the kids to Chicago to be cared for by our sister-in-law, and Darla, of course, stepped right up to the plate saying that she could easily play the role of "Michele" at the resort. We had no doubt this was the case. But that still left us with the need for a replacement "Mike." So, he called up a man who lived in another town who had invited himself to the resort many, many times over the years to play disc golf, and always helped out when he was around.

"Can you come up and be me for the weekend?" asked Mike.

"Sure," he said. "But who's going to be Michele?"

"Well, uh, Darla, of course."

"Great," he beamed. "Does it mean I get to sleep with her?"

That wasn't a joke. We thought it was, but unfortunately it wasn't.

Everything went well at the resort while we were in Colorado, but from that weekend on Darla had a boyfriend. During the week when he was back at home and work, he called to speak to her, and more likely to us, as she was off on other cleaning jobs. He spoke to us like he was our new best friend.

"Do you think Darla likes me?" he asked. "Does she talk about me?"

Since at that time Darla and I didn't talk about much beyond cleaning and what needed to be done around the resort, I was unnerved by the questions.

I'm Living Your Dream Life

"Let's get one thing straight," I said to him. "Darla is *not* my girlfriend. She's my employee. I'm afraid you're going to have to ask her whether or not she likes you."

This wasn't exactly true. During the first years of her employment, Darla and I often shared books, saw a movie together once, and discussed things like antiques and decorating decisions. But I was trying to make a strong point to the new boyfriend. I had already learned the lesson about employee's significant others.

Of course Darla liked him. And during every weekend that followed my friend's Colorado wedding until our departure for Arizona, we ended up with another roommate spending time on Fridays through Mondays in our kitchen, drinking our coffee, giving us advice and judging our lifestyle. Actually, we were happy for Darla. It was probably a terrible experience for her living in our home, relegated to the lower level living quarters. We're a loud, messy family with music and TVs blaring, and a non-stop parade of houseguests. With her own guest around, she was happier and even more exuberant than usual. And we liked the idea of knowing that she wouldn't be completely alone during the winter, even though she had managed beautifully the year before.

But then over the winter she got into an accident while driving our truck. She called us the day it happened and admitted that it was her fault.

"The roads were snowy and I just didn't see the guy," she said. "I wasn't far from home, and was just coming back from another cleaning job." Poor Darla was shaken up but not hurt. She apologized and said she'd take care of everything per our written agreement regarding her use of the truck.

A few weeks later, we received a notice from the other vehicle operator's insurance agent estimating around $3,000 in damage. The estimates on our car were the same. With such high figures there was no way we wanted to make her pay this kind of money. And by law we were required to contact our insurance agent about the claim. In the end we thought the fairest thing for all parties was to file a claim on our insurance to fix both vehicles and have Darla pay the $500 deductible. I knew if I had ever gotten into an accident with someone's car, I would at least offer to pay the insurance deductible. Darla agreed and was grateful to us for being so understanding.

We were just thankful no one was hurt. That was a road we didn't want to travel down again. But sometimes a car out of control has a way of steering itself down roads where you don't want to go, regardless of how hard you drag your heels to try and make it stop. In other words, the boyfriend got involved.

"I can't believe you're going to make Darla pay the deductible on your insurance," he said. "Besides, I don't think the accident was her fault and we're going to court to prove it."

The short story is they went to court. They lost. It *was* her fault.

His next phone call began with a proclamation of his role as a licensed insurance person—or something like that—and that it was his duty to inform us that "in the state of Wisconsin, it is illegal for employers to hold employees responsible for accidents that occurred while on the job and using company vehicles."

"I'm sure you're right," I said, "but in this case the car she was driving was not a company vehicle and she wasn't using it while working for us. We have a separate agreement for the car where not only did we indicate that it was solely for her personal use, but also that she would be responsible for any damage she caused to it. She signed the agreement and she already said she thought paying the deductible was fair."

This turned out to be the second time we were accused of not paying enough for the job—not by the person we hired, but by the person who loved her and claimed he would have to foot the bill for the deductible.

Ah yes, love can be expensive. It can be as expensive as having employees in your life when their personal business becomes your own. I had no intention of backing down on our agreement to have her pay the insurance deductible. It was a matter of principle.

By the way, when we received word from Darla some time later that she had finally given birth to a healthy child, we sent her a symbolic $500 savings bond for the baby. We remain on good terms with her and always think of her fondly.

As for the boyfriend, well, he sent an e-mail calling us greedy and short-sighted, and accused us of taking advantage of his lady. I probably should have kept the twenty-something page typed letter he sent to us after I typed a few choice words back at him through the impersonal world of cyberspace. In fact I probably should have read past the first paragraph before tossing it into the trash as it may have provided some good material for this chapter. But the day it came in the mail, thick as a summons and without a return address, neither Mike nor I were in the mood to be bitch-slapped by anyone.

It was another case of someone seeing only everything we have and nothing we do to pay for it. Even if you give the hired help an expensive car to drive and a beautiful house in which to live (on top of wages for tasks performed), for some, it will never be enough.

If the business is like your child, employees are like stepchildren. They're part of the package and you must learn to deal with them as best you can. Sometimes there may be an actual blood relation with the hired help, such as the series of nephews we've taken on over the years who we fondly call our "whipping-boys." They stay from two weeks to a month during the summer and we house them in a slanted-ceiling room above our living room called "the whipping-boy loft." Like most teenagers, they prefer to sleep until noon and stay up late at night. But we "whip" them into shape by crawling up the ladder to the loft and rouse them from teenage slumber by yelling "get up and rake the beach!"

It seems that for every one person who wishes you well there is at least one—maybe several more—who secretly hopes you'll fall flat on your face. And you have to be very careful about the people you hire to help you along the way. At some point they may just stick out their big, uh, foot, and try to trip you along the way. Other small business owners sing a similar tune when it comes to staff. The tune includes the occasional lucky lyrics like "hard-working and cheerful," but more often words like "ungrateful, late, indolent and envious" arise. The chorus, however, is always the same. It's got a simple beat, you can almost dance to it, and it goes like this: "Good help is hard to find."

My So Called Dream Life

When I was a college student living in southern Illinois, every once in awhile I took a break by visiting a friend or my sister at another university, or went home to see my parents and do my laundry. Each time I made the return trip to school, I remember the overwhelming feeling that stirred inside me when I saw the exit sign on the interstate leading to Carbondale. It caused me to take a deep breath and think, "get ready, 'cause here we go again." Being a college student, one who studied *and* partied, was simply exhausting. Between full-time classes and extracurricular activities and sports, my student job at the newspaper, lots of concerts, friends, roommates and parties, it was a non-stop, twenty-four-hour exercise. Even when I slept it was usually with an open book across my chest. We used to call it "studying by osmosis." College was the place where I learned that my life was in a constant state of run.

My degree is in journalism. Today that only means that I have what my husband calls "a sheepskin," or a framed statement of this fact hanging on the wall somewhere. At this point I'm not sure where it hangs.

I was one of the lucky ones who didn't spend the first few years of college wandering from building to building looking for the office of the major-of-the-month club. I knew from the time I was in elementary school that I wanted to "be" a writer. I received my first five-year diary when I was in fifth grade, and kept a faithful log of my daily events for many years. It started out with handwriting covered in baby fat—lots of loopy loops and circles dotting the i's—and recorded simple things like "went to school, went to bed." Each year the handwriting grew a little tighter, and I found I had more important things to write about—my crush on the cutest boy in class, or my concern with our losing volleyball team. When the five years were up I graduated to bigger, annual books and started calling them journals. Then, as part of my high school journalism class I saw the movie *All the President's Men*, and I knew I'd someday become a journalist as inquisitive and sexy as Robert Redford or Dustin Hoffman.

My parents paid for my first year of college, but told me if I wanted to continue I was on my own. Because of these financial limitations, I had to choose a school I could afford, which translated to "instate college." Carbondale seemed like the right town for me because it was as far away from Chicago as I could get, and it was in the woods. My freshman dorm was located at a place called Thompson Point, which was on a lake. And when my parents moved to Missouri at the same time I finished my freshman year, suddenly they lived only two hours away by car. But since I was serious about school and had decent grades, I had my sights set on what some called the "top journalism school in the country," which just happened to be the University of Missouri in Columbia. With my parents now living in Missouri, I qualified for instate tuition by my junior year, or when the journalism program began. I applied while still a freshman at SIU and was accepted, provided I followed the J-school curriculum set up by the University of Missouri.

It was a traditional liberal arts education with lots of history, rhetoric, foreign language and basic general studies in science, math, economics and government. The program prepares students to dabble in any topic, just as any journalist might be assigned to write a story on any subject at any time, and communicate a modicum of knowledge about the topic in between quotes from the experts in a limited number of words.

I made the move to the Big U at the start of my junior year, but hated it there. The town was too big, the classes were too big and I was a lost soul who didn't know a single other soul. Also, I couldn't find a student job and I needed to work in order to eat. For two weeks I was stuffed in the back room of a small apartment, where I had to walk through the bedroom of another girl, a girl who's name I can't remember, but I do remember she drove a chartreuse Corvette. At the end of the second week I was twenty-five pounds under weight, and severely depressed. I missed my friends back in Carbondale and the place I had learned to call home. So, I packed everything back up in my beloved white '63 Dodge Dart named "Seashell," and headed back to the small, woodsy town of Carbondale, Illinois. Luckily, they accepted me back and that's where I finished my degree. I knew then that I'd probably never make it as a big-time journalist, living in some city, competing for a story or fighting for print space. But in the years that followed, I managed to find jobs in the field and supported myself quite nicely. Almost all the jobs I had were in small office settings.

In the early 1990s, when I worked as a graphic artist and newspaper columnist and before I went to Africa, it never occurred to me that I should be doing something else. At that point doing graphics was my bread and butter, but for a former editor and wannabe writer, it was pretty heady stuff to type seven-hundred words on any subject that came to me in the shower, and have it published on the front page of the Life section each week. I might have been bragging about it one day or something—or maybe I admitted that I was only paid twenty bucks a column—I don't exactly remember what I was talking about the day my father-in-law stood up in a room full of people and said, "If you're such a good writer, then why aren't you rich?"

It felt like a bee sting when he said it—sharp and venomous—and it continued to itch long after the bee died. It came from a self-made businessman, a man I loved and admired, and another person who defined people by what they do instead of who they are, and how much money they make instead of what they do with what they have. It dawned on me that I had probably reached the pinnacle of my journalism career, since I couldn't really see past the Life page of that community newspaper.

People ask me all the time if I miss writing since giving up my job at the newspaper to operate the resort. And it's easy to say no. Since in addition to my less faithful but periodic journal writing, I still write letters to my friends and proposals to sponsors for our disc golf tournaments, as well as promotional materials and communications to our guests.

As for Mike, he hasn't really given up the stock market, either. While at the resort it's nearly impossible for him to keep up with the Dow or the Nasdaq numbers, but when we're in the off-season and staying in Tucson he keeps a running tape of his accounts parading across the bottom of his computer all day. And each time I walk into the bedroom, the TV is tuned to CNBC with more tapes streaming across the screen. He doesn't like the term "day trader," because he says that's for people who buy and sell a lot of things in the same day; but whatever he wants to call himself, he does pretty well with his investments, which is mainly what continues to support our duel lifestyle in Wisconsin and Arizona.

The truth is, it's our life in Tucson that is the dream life. While I still manage the resort by answering the toll free phone, making and confirming reservations, managing the web site, and wading through the never-ending piles of paperwork that includes bills and reports, for the most part I consider myself to be a full-time mom. I get up each morning before six o'clock, which isn't so bad since I usually go to bed shortly after my kids each night at eight or eight-thirty. I put on the coffee (these days it's de-caf), and prepare the only breakfast my girls will eat, which is currently cereal without milk, a glass of orange juice, a gummie bear multivitamin and a chewable Echinacea tablet (it's cold season). Then I check my e-mail, get dressed and make lunches before rousing the girls to get them fed, dressed and out the door. After the bus comes, Wilma Flintstone and I take a three mile walk and talk about everything it means to be a mom and a wife and a sister and a friend, and then until school gets out I'm a free agent.

On the days when I'm not wading through the build-up of sippy cups, laundry, crayons, art projects, books, beads, and stray socks under the kid's beds, or buried in paperwork because no matter what dream life you make for yourself paperwork will always be a part of it, Mike and I play ball golf and disc golf together, shop for groceries or make trips to the hardware store or Home Depot or even the mall. The only shopping we do in Wisconsin is for groceries, and we never do it together. We, in fact, don't do much together when we're there since we're so busy. But in Arizona we coach soccer together, attend church together, and get the kids to tennis and piano lessons without a division of labor, and all with the intention we had when we first bought Sandy Point Resort. And that is going through the everyday motions of our lives *together*.

When spring comes and we find ourselves busy every weekend getting together with friends who we know we won't see for several months when we return to the resort, life starts sprinting again and it trains us for what lies ahead during the summer. And just like I did years earlier upon seeing that sign on the Interstate, I sigh, as I prepare for the ensuing twenty-four-hour exercise. Going to the resort is not at all like going on vacation. It's the most all-encompassing and difficult job I've ever had.

There are times when we actually hate it there.

In the spring of 2001, we hit rock bottom. We returned to the resort six weeks prior to Memorial Day weekend, which is our big opening each season. It's also the weekend that we host one of our two annual PDGA-sanctioned disc golf tournaments, the team tournament. So not only do we need to prepare the cabins and the grounds, we also have to make sure the disc golf course is in top condition and all the tournament scorecards and paperwork are in order. Two new cabins and a new recreation cottage, which began construction over the winter after we tore down the original cabin two and five, and the existing recreation cottage because of its imploding roof, were destined to make their debut that weekend. One of the cabins was ready, but the other wasn't and the recreation cottage still looked like a construction site, polluted with cigarette butts and soda bottles from the workers, as well as nails and scraps of wood everywhere.

Those were probably the worst six weeks of my life. I used the term, "rock bottom," likening it to the addiction of alcoholism, because it was a severe case of workaholism. In addition, I downed quite a bit of Chardonnay after working in and around the cabins and behind the computer for over twenty hours each day, only to pretend to sleep for four or even two hours a night. I wondered whether or not the alcoholic gene my family carries was rearing its ugly head. Whatever it was rearing, it warned me that things like priorities were a bit out of whack. With no child-care program available until June, computer games and PBS kids babysat my children, and I practically threw food at them as I walked by every half-hour or so.

When the building inspector came to the property around the first of May and shut us down for ten days for not obtaining the proper demolition permits, I watched Mike tumble into verbal fits of anger and disappointment, bluntly crying out, "I hate my life." He echoed the feelings I not only uttered from time to time, but also believed in the small silences of my world. The silences I craved and only seemed to find in a short, hot shower every couple days, or if I was lucky, an uninterrupted stint on the toilet in my private bathroom with the birds eye view of the resort. That little space is my aerie, where I hide out and either whip off a crossword puzzle or stare outside pretending no one knows I'm there.

It was overwhelming. Once we were up and running again, with an even tighter deadline, the workers showed up on property at seven in the morning and hammered and sawed and screeched their way through hours of what seemed like minimal progress. Weeks behind schedule, our frustration was mirrored in their faces as they at some point stopped greeting me with a smile or a mere glance. Their boss, our contractor, stopped showing his face on property after the day he came and asked for an additional $30,000 cash without completing the job, and without presenting a single invoice for time and materials. On that same day, when guests were scheduled to arrive in the unfinished cabin, he let out a giant sigh when I suggested he not leave before he at least put door handles on the outside doors of the cabin. It was bad enough that instead of a hardwood floor, the guests had to walk around on pink parchment paper strapped down with duct tape.

"Can't you just have Mike do it?" he asked.

"You don't get it," I said, "I'm not asking you for a favor."

After missing the first one (not having the buildings completed by the tournament), by the final deadline we were ready. On the first Saturday facing a full house that would last for the next eleven weeks, and the first guests to see a new resort, I had only two cabins to clean. Except for the fridges and a few bathroom trash can liners, the rest were ready. I drove around on my golf cart armed with a bottle of bleach and a rag, ready to attack any missed spots of imperfection. As I put myself out there for all to judge, I thought at the very least, let them judge me clean.

Our "new" resort was a big hit, and we had a very successful season. By the last week in August, we were one hundred percent booked for the following summer. We had crawled from the pit of construction and debt, and composed a letter to our guests explaining that it was time to raise our rates.

In spite of everything that's happened in the last decade, I can still think back to the first time I saw Sandy Point Resort and it's easy to remember why we bought it. Seeing the resort for the first time reminds me of the first time I ever saw Mike. He doesn't remember meeting me, and he says I don't remember meeting him. Apparently we met each other at different times. But I distinctly remember the men's clothing store where he worked for a short time in Evanston, Illinois and the day my college roommate brought me there to meet him. They were good friends and grew up together in the same neighborhood, and until college went to the same schools. Mike doesn't remember meeting me then, because I think all he saw was his old friend loudly bursting into the otherwise quiet store and calling attention to him. How he doesn't remember seeing me that day is baffling. After all, I wore two-inch heels and when I wear heels I'm hard to miss. I guess on that afternoon I just wasn't his type.

The first thing I thought when I saw Mike was that he was beautiful.

Too beautiful for the likes of me. Besides, he was dating a friend of mine, a girl who lived in my dorm. And since he barely looked up to acknowledge me that day in the store, I knew he wasn't interested. I didn't know for several years and a lot of time spent getting to know one another, that he was the one for me or even that we had potential to be a couple. But I do remember I liked what I saw. Mike, by the way, recalls meeting me for the first time at a later date in his old girlfriend's dorm room when he was visiting our school. He not only thought I was tall, but also that I was stuck up. Now *that* I believe.

When I first saw Sandy Point Resort, there was no question that it was a beautiful spot. Even though we had searched all day for a place to buy, it was hardly a long-term, exhaustive search. Joining hands with it was all pretty whimsical. Calling ourselves resort owners was something we knew we could accomplish quickly and easily, merely by writing a check. Calling ourselves resort operators could only come years after walking down that eighty-five-foot dock and saying, "I do." Just as our marriage evolved to include two children and a home in Tucson and a relationship that continues to improve as it ages, the resort has become a part of us, as each year we make our mark by improving and changing it. It's like our third child, a child of whom we are very proud. Obviously, it has presented numerous challenges.

It's been said over and over that the most difficult job in the world is the job of raising children. As a parent, I know it can also be the most rewarding. And so it goes for the job as resort owner and operator. I wrote in earlier chapters about the jerks who sometimes come to our resort, and also about the problems we've had with our staff over the years. Again, I can't help but think there's something wrong with the way the negative stories seem to get all the attention, especially when there are so many truly wonderful things about our life at the resort. And the majority of our guests who come year after year are wonderful people.

We have one family of regular guests who has christened four genera-

I'm Living Your Dream Life

tions off the shores of the beach at Sandy Point. Grandpa started coming in the early days in the 1930s. Then he brought his son, who later brought his wife and three children. Now two of those children bring children we've watched grow from babies to adolescents, and the third child has become an avid disc golfer after putting down his fishing pole one day and picking up a golf disc. When we met this family for the first time, it was during our second month of operation and when only the original five cabins stood. Unaware of the family's extensive history at the resort, when we started the check-in procedure I told them what to expect in their cabins.

"Actually, cabin number three is the warmest," interrupted the mother, "and number one has the best cross-breeze. Number two has critters living in the walls and number five has a leaky roof."

She was absolutely correct. I wondered what else she could tell me and thought about taking out my notepad.

This family was the first to stay in the first two cabins we built, which we "finished" about fifteen minutes before their arrival during our second season of operation. That morning both units still looked very much like construction sites, with scraps of lumber, nails, screws, bits of screen and shingles strewn about. And even though there were a lot of undotted i's and uncrossed t's in the form of missing trim and a completely stocked kitchen, they were very understanding and complementary of our work. They left us with a new cast iron frying pan as a cabin-warming gift, with a note that said fishermen can't cook without one.

A few years into our tenure, grandpa passed away. They wrote to tell us the sad news and then his son called to ask if we would be willing to accept as a gift Grandpa's prize trophy fish, a thirty-six-pound, fifty-one-inch mounted muskie captured in Squaw Lake back in 1970. "The fish's name is George," said his son, "and we would very much like to see him go home." We were flattered by the offer and have now proudly displayed George in a prominent spot in our front office/pro shop. It adds the question, "Did that fish come out of this lake?" to our list of F.A.Q.'s each summer.

They were also among the first to stay in the last cabin we built, the one that greeted its first guests with the pink parchment paper. We had one week after the tournament to get the floor in and the screen porch built before the next guests arrived, but those weren't the only factors. In our rush to clean and furnish the cabin, because of our nightmare experience with the contractor, we noticed only minutes before the first guests were due to arrive that some incompetent boob on the work-crew had left an open can of purple-pipe glue on the bottom of the fiberglass tub. Cardboard and sawdust, scraps of wood paneling and insulation had covered it, so we didn't see it until the last minute. The result was a giant black hole in the middle of the tub, where the glue ate the fiberglass. The black and blue mark appeared impossible to fix. But since the hole didn't go all the way through to the floor, we simply covered it with a bath mat and warned the guests. I imagined having to do that each week all summer long, and hoped we wouldn't be judged too harshly.

But our favorite family, a family who happens to be in the construction business, came up with a quick and easy solution that did not involve tearing out the tub and shower unit from behind the wood paneled walls.

"Why don't you just call in a fiberglass repair person to do it?" they said. "In this town where there are so many boat repair businesses, surely you'll be able to find someone."

They, of course, were right, and happily allowed the repairman into their cabin during their week's stay, and agreed not to use the shower/tub for the required twenty-four-hour period of time. They also let us come in and hang the mini blinds in their kitchen and living room windows.

After putting so much sweat, time and money, and so many hopes into this place, we can't help but believe it's going to continue to get better. We're finally in the black, and that sure helps. It took far too long.

When I was in elementary school I walked to and from school every day along the same path. From the front door of the school to my back door, a sidewalk cut into four-foot squares led my way. Usually I walked with a friend or my sister and we talked about things like bell-bottom pants and what Elvis movie was showing on TV for the 3:30 pm movie. Along the path was a chain link fence, a fence that enclosed a typical suburban backyard. It was the home of a black and brown dog named Susie. While I usually stopped to pet this friendly dog, first by sticking my hands through the fence and as I grew older and taller by reaching over the top, one day I walked alone I noticed Susie was not outside. Looking for a friend, I called her name and stood there for a while, hoping she'd come bounding toward the fence to greet me. But she didn't come. I remember thinking how strange it felt that I was not only walking home alone, but that my regular routine of saying hello to Susie was interrupted. But without Susie or anyone else to distract me, I looked around the yard and the street next to me and noticed how very peaceful it all was. I took a deep breath, and knew at that moment I was a happy person.

"Remember this," I said out loud. "Remember this moment."

I have moments like that at the resort all the time. Even with a full house I often find time alone where I take in those medicinal, deep breaths and really appreciate the beauty of everything around me. The lane going from our front door to the boundary of the property where the sign is located and where we collect our mail is about a quarter mile long. It's a walk I enjoy making twice a day, first to take out the mail, and second to bring home the incoming mail. Often I take Willow and Camille, and we've had many treasure hunts along the way. These beautiful little girls buzz around me from one side of the road to the other, scooping up fascinating leaves, sticks and birch bark, or perfect wild flowers and colorful berries to add to their baskets.

"Here's a treasure," they say. "Here's another treasure. Is this a treasure?" As their baskets fill up with nature's goodies, they hand them to me to carry the rest of the way home. Then they trot off to chase feathers floating in the breeze or marvel at butterflies, caterpillars and toads. I watch them as though they move in slow motion, and the never-ending chorus of bird calls that fill the air from just before sunrise to just after sunset each day drowns out my thoughts.

Sometimes at night after we put the kids to bed and we still have enough energy left to find each other and recap the day, Mike and I take a flashlight and go for a walk around the property. We call it the nightly "rounds," and we do what we can to go unnoticed by the guests. We walk arm-in-arm and talk about the day or sometimes we don't talk at all as we silently chuckle about the fact that together we've been doing this thing called Sandy Point Resort for so many years now. Other nights, when we have a lot of pent-up energy, we take a set of glow-in-the-dark discs and a couple glow sticks with us and shoot a round of night golf. It seems we both end up posting better scores at night and believe we should probably play during the day with our eyes closed.

When daylight comes again and the girls are up and ready to rush outside to swim in the lake or play on the playground, I follow them outside and take in the pungent, clean smell of pine. Pushing them on the swings of our playground, I feel hypnotized by their back and forth motion, and I imagine them growing up. I see them going from tiny babies born in the forest to barefoot little girls chasing chipmunks and collecting rocks. The curls on their heads stretch into braids and toothless grins grow into exuberant smiles and joyous laughter. I see the wonderful backdrop we've provided for their childhood and the endless parade of friends who come to play with them week after week each summer.

Truly, we *have* created a dream life.

About the Author

Michele VanOrt Cozzens, along with her husband and two daughters, divides her time between the Northwoods of Wisconsin and Tucson, Arizona. The owner/operator of Sandy Point Resort and Disc Golf Ranch since 1993, she is a former newspaper columnist for a community newspaper group in the San Francisco Bay Area. And although she no longer competes, she is still registered in the pro master women's division of the Professional Disc Golf Association and continues to act as a tournament director and promoter of the sport.